Praise for *Scale or Fail*

"Don't be an entrepreneur who settles. Growth takes persistence and an unwillingness to take no for an answer. *Scale or Fail* is the secret sauce to help you overcome setbacks and win big."

—**Barbara Corcoran**, founder of
The Corcoran Group, author, and Shark Tank investor

"By reading *Scale or Fail*, you are taking the important first step toward building a bigger, better, and stronger business. This book helps you look deep within yourself to be able to identify your superhero strengths, focus on them, train others to do what you do – and then let go to move on to your next potential multi-million dollar enterprise. This is not an easy task for anyone to accomplish, and we are lucky to have Allison's book by our side to support us along the way!"

—**Dean Graziosi**, entrepreneur, real estate expert, and
New York Times bestselling author

"Allison is brilliant at taking huge complex ideas and breaking them down into small, simple steps that anyone can follow. If you want to learn how to grow and scale your business whilst feeling empowered and happy (because both are important!) then buy, read, and implement this book now. You won't need another business book for a decade."

—**Geeta Sidhu-Robb**, CEO, Nosh Detox,
Entrepreneur of the Year, London 2017

"If you have a small business and want to do something spectacular with it, you need to visualize several years down the road what it will look like and then translate it into a clear picture for your team. The invaluable tools in this book will help take that vision and turn the scaling rollercoaster into the ride of your life."

—**Cameron Herold**, founder of COO
Alliance and author of *Double Double* and *Vivid Vision*

"Allison Maslan draws on the wisdom of building 10 companies to give you her revolutionary method towards building a self-managed company. *Scale or Fail* turns confusion into clarity and condenses what you need to know in a way that can be applied immediately. Gift this to every business owner you know that is serious about taking the leap!"

—**Roland Frasier**, serial entrepreneur, attorney, and Principal
of Digital Marketer and CEO of War Room

"I've often said, 'Life gives to the giver and takes from the taker.' Allison Maslan is an awesome giver who has written the new authority book on scaling. She totally speaks my language, especially when it comes to networking, providing sound marketing advice, and advising business owners on how to let go of what is not excellent and driving the long-term vision. This book can help you be the first domino in several chains of dominoes."

—**Joe Polish**, founder and President,
Piranha Marketing Inc., and Genius Network

"When you are looking for a business mentor, find one that has been there and done it. In Allison's book, *Scale or Fail*, Allison not only shares her top growth strategies, she shares her wisdom from being in the trenches year after year. She knows what works and what does not in todays new economy. Give your scale journey a shortcut and read her groundbreaking book. Your life will never be the same."

—**Michael Bernoff**, Founder and CEO of
Human Communications Institute

"As you dive deeper into your business growth, the sky is the limit. However, most entrepreneurs find themselves hitting a wall at some point and forgetting all the incredible possibilities that their business can create. Allison's book *Scale or Fail* literally removes that wall by showing you step-by-step how to scale to your Pinnacle one big leap at a time."

—**Christina Rassmussen**, founder of Life Reentry
Institute and bestselling author of
Second Firsts: Live, Laugh, and Love Again

"If you have a business that you want to scale but it (and you) don't have the systems to scale it to becoming an enterprise or a valuable asset you can sell someday, Allison Maslan is for you. I believe the best way to judge a businessperson is to meet her clients and see what happens in her community. Allison attracts high-quality professionals who are implementers. They love Allison. She's impeccable and so is her business. She's married to an amazing man, she's a mom, and she's surround by wonderful friends who love and care about her.... If you're looking for a mentor who walks the walk and lives the life she promises that you can have too, then Allison is the missing piece in your puzzle. She's the whole package with a model that can work for you."

—**Mike Koenigs**, CEO, You Everywhere Now, and
author of thirteen bestsellers, including
Publish and Profit and *Money Phone*

"There are entrepreneurs who make money, there are entrepreneurs who change the world, and there are icons who do both! Allison Maslan is that icon! When it comes to business mentors and coaches there is no one better. I highly recommend Allison Maslan to any business or entrepreneur seeking proven results."

—**Vince Reed**, founder, Internet Traffic
Factory and Set Up My Ads

"Heyo, Fire Nation! If you want to take your business to the next level, you need to be productive, be disciplined, have focus – and read Allison Maslan's *Scale or Fail*. This book gets you out of your comfort zone, which is a dangerous place to live. I keep saying: Disappointment is a possible result of every action. But what's the result of no action? Nothing. If you really want to do something and accomplish it right away, start now by following Allison's guidance."

—**John Lee Dumas (aka JLD)**, founder and
host, *Entrepreneurs On Fire* podcast

"As a Digital Marketer since 1995 (that's BG – Before Google), I now know 'START-UP' and 'SCALE-UP' requires two different skill sets. The book you hold in your hands teaches both in elegant, simple-to-understand lessons. As you'll read through these pages, Allison Maslan really created a 'how to' course worth several hundred dollars – not just a book you can get for less than $25 on Amazon! Although you and I are probably perfect strangers, I hope one day I'll read in the news about how this book helped you 'scale' your business and sell it for millions. Until then, I encourage you to read it *twice* – once for 'literacy' (learning) and a second time for 'fluency' (mastery). Friend: read these pages carefully because they could change your personal and professional life forever!"

—**Alex Mandossian**, founder and CEO,
All Selling Aside

SCALE
OR
FAIL

HOW TO BUILD YOUR DREAM TEAM,

EXPLODE YOUR GROWTH,

AND LET YOUR BUSINESS SOAR

Allison Maslan

WILEY

Library of Congress Cataloging-in-Publication Data:

Names: Maslan, Allison, author.
Title: Scale or fail : how to build your dream team, explode your growth,
   and let your business soar / Allison Maslan.
Description: Hoboken, New Jersey : Wiley, [2018] |
Identifiers: LCCN 2018020269 (print) | LCCN 2018036056 (ebook) | ISBN
   9781119461043 (Adobe PDF) | ISBN 9781119461036 (ePub) | ISBN 9781119461012
   | ISBN 9781119461012 (hardcover) | ISBN 9781119461043 (ePDF) | ISBN
   9781119461036 (ePub)
Subjects: LCSH: New business enterprises–Management. | Business planning.
Classification: LCC HD62.5 (ebook) | LCC HD62.5 .M3656 2018 (print) | DDC
   658.1/1–dc23
LC record available at https://lccn.loc.gov/2018020269

Printed in the United States of America

V10004143_083118

Dedicated to you,
the Enterprising Entrepreneur,
whose gifts the world needs.
May this book give you the wings to fly.

Fearlessness is like a muscle. I know from my own life that the more I exercise it, the more natural it becomes to not let my fears run me. The first time we take that first fearless step, we begin to change our lives. And the more we act on our dreams and our desires, the more fearless we become.

—Arianna Huffington

Contents

Make decisions from where you are going, not from where you are at.
—Allison Maslan

How This Book Is Different

There are many books available that share and teach principles that will help you grow or scale your company. Often the reader completes one of these books feeling inspired and motivated, but then becomes perplexed on what steps to actually take to reach their goals and how to apply them to their own business. What sets *Scale or Fail* apart is that I am not merely sharing my philosophy with you on how you can scale your business. In these pages, I also teach you step-by-step how to utilize the SCALEit Method® to fast track your success, growth, and profits. It's easy to follow, workable, and so valuable.

You are not simply holding in your hands a book that offers great insights. You are about to read a complete, signature program that will transform your company beyond your wildest dreams.

Foreword

When you first meet Allison, you get the sense that she has done impossible things. This feeling is not easily articulated. It is an unspoken energy that surrounds her. It is an invisible, powerful force that comes through in such a gentle way that you want to take on the hardship of scaling. She has a way with it, and she teaches you not only how to scale, but also how to scale over and over again.

You see, she takes that invisible force and gives it to you. At first she makes you feel that it is easy to do – that it is possible for you to overcome all the pain, all the fear, all the uncertainty. You even forget that scaling is daunting. This is how it felt when I first met her in 2011. I was just starting out with my Life Reentry work and she grabbed my hand and said, "Christina, this will be hard, but you can do this." I remember thinking: *I know what hard is, this can't be harder than loss.* After all, I had lost my husband and had gone through some impossible things. But she was right, it was close.

Scaling is brutal. It is not for the faint of heart. It is as painful and as impossible as the hardest things in life. It requires something, a very important something: *resilience to pain.* You have an opponent every day when you wake up. Your opponent is called *struggle.* You have to fight with *struggle* every day and, in the end, you must win.

Somehow, Allison has won tens of thousands of these battles with her gentle fierceness. She built 10 businesses and has held the hand of so many like myself who were starting out and showed them what is possible. I know you want to change the world. I know you have a dream – a mission, a fire inside of you that wants to create, grow, and scale it to reach millions of people.

Well, you have the right book in your hands to help make this a reality.

It doesn't matter what business you are in. You may have created a hair salon because of the way you believe women should feel about themselves. Or, you have a grocery store that influences the gut health of your customers and you want one in every corner. Maybe you own an engineering company that is ready to innovate your industry or a construction company with a big vision to transform the way we live. This book is made for you.

I have to be honest with you. Scaling your dream is almost impossible. Most of the time the safety net is nonexistent. Nothing is underneath you to catch you, and this is why Allison wrote this book. She built you a net to catch you when you fall. She is here to ensure that you scale and not fail.

I will never forget the day I spent with Allison at her office many years ago. She stood in front of me with a big black marker and a whiteboard and showed me what my work could do for the world. She found the proof I was missing when my struggles and fears would wake me up in the morning waiting for the battle. I saw the vision of what was possible for the first time. In Allison's fashion, she made it seem simple, easy, doable, and you know what else? Fun.

I realized then that the invisible force that surrounded Allison was her ability to have fun even while scaling and doing impossible things. Her vibe, her spirit, and her essence came from her flying in her trapeze every week, no matter how hard her days had been. She has taught herself to fly even on the days that she was falling – maybe even *especially* on those days.

As I read this book I realized that she took all of her flying experience and made it into words so that you too could tap into this invisible force as you find your way to scaling your big dream. As for me, the vision Allison wrote on that whiteboard has come true 10-fold. When you read the book and you apply her formula, your vision will become a bigger and brighter reality than you ever thought possible. Enjoy the flying, the scaling, and changing the world.

I am.

—**Christina Rasmussen**, founder of Life Reentry Institute, and bestselling author of *Second Firsts: Live, Laugh, and Love Again*

Introduction

Oh, what if I fall?
Oh but my darling, what if you fly?

— Erin Hanson, young poet

caling a business has many similarities to swinging on the
flying trapeze. I should know – as an adult, I have learned to
do both.

On the trapeze, you must climb a 35-foot ladder to reach
the top. Yes, it can be terrifying – but, just like growing your
business, you must be willing to take many fearful risks in order
to achieve your goals.

Once you make it up the ladder, you are standing on a
platform that's only a few feet wide. It is nerve wracking and, to
some people, paralyzing. People often allow their fear or lack
of direction to hold them back, and they are not willing to take
the leap.

It is exactly the same in business when you are poised to
expand and scale.

You have two choices at this point. One: You can gather
your courage and break through to where all the riches are
waiting – this experience is exhilarating, enriching, and tremen-
dously rewarding. Or two: You can get stuck on the platform and
tell yourself every reason why scaling is not a good idea. In this
scenario, you go nowhere.

What will you choose to do?

I chose the first option, though it took some time to get there. I started my first business in college and, by the age of 25, I was already running my own national advertising and public relations firm. My clients included Fortune 100 companies such as Supercuts, Ben & Jerry's, and Charlotte Russe. I was making great money, but I was working night and day. I should have been on top of the world, but I had no life of my own and, honestly, I felt miserable.

I recognized that my business needed a new model to continue its growth beyond my own individual efforts, but I didn't know how. Years later, after a powerful wake-up call resulting from a near-fatal car accident and a failing marriage, I made a life-changing decision to walk away from the lucrative agency that was starving my soul and figure out how to get *there* – whatever that ultimately was going to mean.

The result was that I developed an innovative method of scaling that led to a much more impactful and meaningful business path, both personally and monetarily. I took a risk and have never looked back. Instead, I've moved forward to achieve even greater success through building and scaling nine additional businesses, generating millions of dollars. It is of even greater personal importance to me that along the way I've developed a business mentoring company that has helped thousands of other business owners around the world realize their full potential.

As many of us know and have already experienced, dreams can easily get shattered. (If you are among the few who haven't yet, trust me when I say that *you will*. As you'll discover in this book, setbacks and failure *are not a bad thing*.) Expectations sometimes need flexibility, a willingness to look at a challenge from a new set of eyes. Starting out with an innovative idea, seed money, hard work, hope, and confidence-building pep talks are all great assets – but they are certainly not guarantees for success. There are a great many variables affecting whether you and your business reach their full potential.

Growing your business is an even more daunting endeavor. You've made it through the early stages, you've built a client base, you've established some product recognition, you've seen some decent results, and maybe you've even managed to keep your cash flow somewhat consistent. But soon you find that the business is leveling off. Costs are rising. In order to achieve your long-term financial goals, you know you need to expand existing revenue streams or create new ones, or your company will stagnate and then sink. On the other hand, such expansion involves risk. As a rabbi once said to me, when I was discussing the pains of my marriage at that time, "Nothing worth having is ever easy."

However, there are ways that you can stack the odds heavily in your favor. The scaling model described in this book – which has guided the success of many of my clients – is a practical, proactive approach that can also help you to shift your risk–reward equation. You have nothing to lose except a few hours invested in reading this book and applying its methodology.

What Is Scaling, Exactly?

When founders reach a certain point at which they feel as if they are chasing their tails and putting out fires, have unending To Do lists, and never have any free time, it becomes impossible for them to focus on the things that can actually grow their businesses. They've had success with their companies and with building revenue, but they just can't seem to make the jump to the next level or even to hire the right people. It drives them nuts, taking all the wind out of their sales (pun intended!) and the fun out of their lives.

So, what does the word *scaling* mean for those founders – perhaps this group includes you – who can't seem to get to that elusive next level? I like to think of this in terms of being able to grow your business while at the same time managing the expanding workload without sacrificing your level of performance, efficiency, and employee safety. In fact, if you are scaling properly, you are creating processes and workflows that improve all areas of your operation and save you a lot of time, money, and headaches. By adopting a scalable business model, you can generate huge profits without all the budgetary strains that overburden traditional growth models.

The goal of scaling is to build a replicable system for delivering products and services that allow businesses to increase their customer base without having to increase their overhead at the same pace. The traditional growth model has fostered a vicious cycle of inefficiency, causing companies to hit a wall that they cannot break through. For instance, a company gains a few new clients, so they hire more people to service those clients, adding costs at nearly the same rate that they're adding revenue. The method in this book will show you how to grow, replicate, and expand while at the same time building a self-managed company that you can step away from for periods of time as it continues to soar. Most Fortune 500 companies are structured in a way that allows the CEOs to come and go without impacting the company's success. This is a mere dream for most business owners, but in this book I am going to show you exactly how it can become your reality.

To me, successful scaling means that you get to a point in your business where you are flying higher with less effort and resistance – like a professional trapeze artist who creates more height, power, and momentum when he allows the physics of his leap, swing, and team to carry him to new heights. Let me explain how this concept works.

Scaling Away with the Greatest of Ease

Let's start with a story, to illustrate my philosophy of scaling and how I find a great metaphor in the exhilarating world of trapeze artistry.

Years ago, when I was at a crossroads in my life, I happened upon the Flying Gaonas – a fifth-generation family of trapeze artists who performed with circuses such as the Ringling Bros. and Barnum & Bailey's Circus and the Big Apple Circus. Richie Gaona, a legendary trapeze artist himself, operates a training facility called Gaona's Trapeze Workshop, where people from all over the globe are trained to "fly."

Now, having been a gymnast back in high school, I became exhilarated at the prospect of trying out this physical – and seemingly dangerous – art form. I simply *had* to try this out for myself and take the leap, as it were. From that very first leap, I was hooked.

More than 18 years later and still going strong, I continue to climb up that 35-foot ladder to a narrow pedestal and stretch out into the air. In my mind I visualize the routine ahead of me as well as my safe landing, sometimes reciting to myself the lyrics from the song "The Daring Young Man on the Flying Trapeze" – probably the most famous circus song ever, and written as a tribute to real-life nineteenth-century French trapeze artist Jules Léotard.

Below, a team of flyers and spectators watch with anticipation as I inch my toes to the edge of the platform. I draw in and release a deep breath and, an instant later, jump into midair. I somersault once ... then twice (that is the plan) and, with the goal of just the right timing and finesse, clasp my arms gracefully with those of another trapeze artist, who is appropriately known as the *catcher*. And, because a trapeze artist should always seek to take her aerial feats to the next level, I repeat all of this motion again – only this time with a jump that is higher up, a swing with more drive, or an additional twist to push myself beyond what I thought I was capable of achieving. The goal in business and trapeze arts is to surpass what your mind wants you to believe you can accomplish while assembling the systems, processes, and team behind you so that you can soar. Like any team sport, it is the union of the individual's determination, persistence, and finesse, intertwined with the right strategies and team to propel from.

Okay, my feet are now firmly back on earth. You are no doubt still wondering: What does all of this have to do with scaling? As it turns out, scaling a business shares a similar process to swinging on a trapeze – although of course it's all planted on the ground.

Playing It Safe Isn't a Business Strategy

As a businessperson, you must develop a clear vision, stretch yourself into unchartered territories, and sync gracefully with the right team. In both instances, tremendous amounts of fear are typically involved.

Because the scaling process and fear of the unknown and/ or failure are so daunting and scary, business owners are often unwilling to take the leaps necessary to take their businesses to the next level and grow. And yet, calculated risk-taking is an essential part of success, which means that avoiding the scaling process due to fear of failure will completely paralyze and stagnate your business. This book is less about the prudence of weighing risk and reward – which, to be sure, is just plain smart to do – and more about failure caused by surrendering to the irrational fears, disorganized thought processes, and blindness to life-changing opportunities in favor of the status quo.

> Avoiding danger is no safer in the long run than outright exposure. The fearful are caught as often as the bold.
> —*Helen Keller, author, activist, and lecturer*

Consider the statistics. The "play it safe" mindset leads *34 million* American business owners to avoid risk entirely and suffer from *smallness*. But what these business owners don't realize is that playing it safe leads to *unsafe* results – missed opportunities, inability to meet demand, lost market-share, flat-to-declining performance, employee unrest and turnover – or, a business that could have been and would have been, yet never made the full commitment to fly, so to speak.

These Titans Flopped Big Time

The great entrepreneurs know that it takes an iron stomach to succeed in business. You must learn from your mistakes – many of them extremely painful – before you can reboot, recharge your courage, and expend your time, energy and, more often than not, invest what little remains of your savings. What I know to be true is that my biggest turnarounds and upswings came when I hit a wall *hard* and was forced to look at the situation creatively with a new set of eyes and devise an innovative solution to not only recover, but to ultimately fly high rather than remain stuck.

For a moment, consider these four mega-flops: an online auction site; a cutting-edge computer; a fried chicken recipe that was rejected some 1,000 times; and a soda product to compete with Coke and Pepsi.

Would you ever guess that, in order, these epic flops were from Jeff Bezos (zShops), Steve Jobs (NeXT Computers), Colonel Sanders (KFC Chicken before it finally clicked), and Richard Branson (Virgin Cola)? I would say that these four all overcame their fears and failures to land just a bit of success, wouldn't you? They persevered regardless of their setbacks. Lesson: Never, ever allow a "No" or a flop to stop you.

Even if such extreme outcomes don't occur, the worst feeling for any entrepreneur is to settle on a shrinking vision – whether you are a fledgling or have been chipping away at it for many years. Chances are you came to this book because you began with *big dreams* and you continue to hold on tight to them. You want to stretch yourself, grow, and soar through the air like a trapeze artist.

I relate to all of this because I used to be one of the many entrepreneurs – perhaps like you at this moment – who was frustrated because I was stuck in overwhelmed mode. Things changed only when l began to stretch myself beyond what I had thought were my limitations. Channeling the same self-assurance I had when I leapt off the platform to catch the trapeze bar with my hands, I catapulted from being a small-time entrepreneur to the leader of a thriving enterprise.

Okay, I've Launched My Business – Now What?

When I was a struggling single mom, I had to get honest real fast about my illusions that I had a business safety net. Instead, I embraced the idea of transforming from an underdog small business owner to a powerhouse CEO. I was not savvy by any means in those early days, but I was smart enough to know what I did not know. I realized that, if I was going to fly into the unknown, I needed to surround myself with experts who had walked the walk before me. Just as I had found a top trapeze coach to help instruct and guide me to successfully fulfill that passion, I recognized I needed to do the same for my business. Looking back, finding the *right advisors* who "had been there, done that" and could give it to me straight was the best strategic move I ever made toward finding long-term success.

It's possible you've heard this advice before in some form or another. In fact, you can find a lot of excellent advice if you are in start-up mode or are in the early stages of owning a business. But there isn't as much help available once your business is off the ground. You may even feel like a forgotten entrepreneur trying to figure it all out on your own and ask yourself: "I made it *here*, but how the heck do I get *there*?"

What I have found from my own personal experience in building 10 successful companies over three decades – each one started from scratch and scaled up – and from sharing my process with thousands of business owners, is that there exists a certain place no one tells you about as you are growing your company. In fact, you may not even recognize you are there until you have been stuck for some time.

Entering Another Dimension

This vast nowhere land resides somewhere in the void between *entrepreneur* and *enterprise*. I liken it to *The Twilight Zone* TV show, except in this case it's where so many small business owners inexplicably get lost and stagnant. To quote a line from the opening monologue of the classic TV series: "It lies between the pit of man's fears and the summit of his knowledge."

> There was nothing in the dark that wasn't there when the lights were on.
> —*Rod Serling, screenwriter, playwright, and narrator of*
> The Twilight Zone

Once you've crossed into the entrepreneurial Twilight Zone, you struggle to find your way out and think you are trapped there forever while fumbling through trying to build an enterprise. After many failed attempts landing you right back where you started, you start to feel like "the little engine that could" from the children's book. When you ride on flat and steady land, you are cruising along. But when you hit the steep hills, you find you need a lot more horsepower, direction, and support in order to reach the top. You have shifted into playing a much bigger game with more pressure and greater responsibility, and it takes so much more resilience and fortitude to obtain a win. As in the Little Engine story, you hear your inner voice chant: "I think I can, I think I can, I think I can …"

"Wait a minute," the voice says to you. "I *don't* think I can. I need larger wheels, a stronger engine, and more *oomph* to keep up with those bigger trains and make it through the entire journey."

You really want to get up that hill – that is, grow your business – but nothing that you did starting out as an early entrepreneur seems to be working anymore – even when you pressed yourself harder. In all likelihood, you have your hands in every part of the business, wearing way too many hats in an effort to maintain control. Meanwhile, you are continuing to implement the same old strategies, management practices, and mindset that you used in the early days – which will not work as you get further along on your climb.

I'll use another classic children's story to illustrate my point. Do you remember in Lewis Carroll's classic *Alice in Wonderland* when Alice blew up like a giant in the White Rabbit's tiny house, with her arms and legs flailing through the doors and windows? When she was smaller, she fit just fine in the little house. Now that she has grown, she is busting out at the seams.

Apply that image to your business situation and you can see why things that used to work before have all of a sudden stopped functioning as expected. Products or services that used to sell are no longer selling. Systems that used to keep you in check are breaking down. Important tasks are slipping through the cracks and you are running around like a crazy person trying to hold it all together. And you are realizing that some of the employees who helped you so much in the beginning don't have the skills or fortitude to take you to the next level.

Here's the thing. You can't build a bigger house upon the same foundation and beams as those of your smaller house. Similarly, you can't double or triple your company's revenue with the same bandwidth, thought processes, tools, and materials you used when you started. Amazon.com, Apple, Google, and even Disney all originated in garages years ago and have long since outgrown them. Imagine if they'd never left their garages – what do you think would have happened? Sticking to old habits is a recipe to fail, not scale, and they are no way to live your life, much less run a company.

That said, it is understandable why so many business owners keep banging their heads against a wall to figure out how to get to the next level while refusing to try anything new or different. We take action based on what we know and what we have done before, as if the past can predict the future. Certainly, there is a lot to be learned from prior experience. However, as is the case when it comes to most habits, it is often not about having learned with an eye toward enrichment, but rather, from unconscious programming that is far removed from any informed decision-making. Obvious examples of this occur all the time in everyday life and you don't even realize it. How many times have you not consumed enough water during exercise and then felt dehydrated? Or how many times have you stayed up late to get work done and then were ragged and red-eyed for an important meeting the next day?

Letting Go of What You Know

In order to recondition your mind with new choices for expansion while you are in the Twilight Zone, chugging up the hill, and shedding your old business model, you must be willing to get out of your comfort zone and let go of everything you've been doing. Just as a trapeze artist must step off the platform and venture into the unknown with a completely different mindset than the one she had while her feet were on the ground, you must also clear your mind before stepping into uncharted territory.

Yes, of course, you should value your life experience and be proud of your acquired wisdom. At the same time, however, you need to be honest with yourself and realize that some of those things might also be holding you back from spring boarding to reach your fullest potential.

To begin, ask yourself these important questions:

- Am I playing big enough?
- Do I look at my business as a way to change the world?
- How big of an impact do I want to make?

Maybe you've heard or read about businesses that skyrocket from $500,000 to $100 million in what seems like record speed. The truth is, in most cases these companies underwent years of strategic planning and blood, sweat, and tears prior to experiencing this astronomical growth. You didn't hear about their grass roots rev-up before their scale-up. No doubt you were also unaware there were also common philosophies, practices, and systems in play among these success stories that helped them overcome their fears, break free from their stagnant thinking, change their limiting habits, and navigate other bumps in the road while they scaled.

The Fastest-Growing Companies

In 2017, *Fortune* announced its annual list of "100 Fastest Companies." What is most striking about this list is that 7 out of the top 10 began as startups created by one or two people and then over the years (seemingly "overnight") found a way to scale to ginormous proportions through a wide range of means (sometimes via investment capital and a company sale or merger). Many of them have sustained and prospered while weathering all kinds of storms over the years, only to come out on top. In most cases, the original founders, such as Mark Zuckerberg and Jeff Bezos, have famously (or infamously, depending on your point of view) continued to maintain control over their megabusinesses.

Among these remarkable success stories: Lending Tree (launched in 1996 by Doug Lebda) at #3; ABIOMED (founded by David M. Lederman in 1981 as Applied Biomedical Corporation) at #4; Facebook (founded by Mark Zuckerberg and Edouardo Saverin in 2004) at #6; Netease (founded by Ding Lei in 1997) at #7; Ellie Mae (founded by Sig Anderman in 1997); Amazon.com (founded in 1995 by Jeff Bezos) at #9; and Arista Networks (originally cofounded in 1982 as Sun Microsystems by Andy Bechtolsheim) at #10.

So, how do these great success stories fit into your vision of where your business is headed? Whether you are going from a local shop to a regional chain or from a national brand to an international household name, the answer will always be the same. In order to take the leap from entrepreneur to enterprise, you must be willing to tear the pieces of your business apart and reconstruct them at a higher level that drives your growth. It doesn't matter whether you are in the six figures and scaling to seven, or seven figures and scaling to eight or even nine, you must be willing to get out of your comfort zone and jump while at each level.

The good news is that there is always a safety net on the trapeze. And, when it comes to scaling, this book will serve as part of your safety net to ensure you manage falls and setbacks, receive all the support you need, and get right back on the trapeze.

Sure, it is scary. But the strategies I provide in this book will help you separate real fears from imagined ones, assess them carefully, and ultimately choose growth over staying still.

Time to Fly!

My intent with *Scale or Fail* is to help business owners and entre-preneurs like you get past the mental and strategic pitfalls that cause revenue bottlenecks and expansion headaches, stunting financial and personal growth. Applying my formula with diligence has led to breakthroughs every day for so many of my clients – from neighborhood sole proprietors to CEOs of nationally known brand-name corporations.

In the chapters that follow, I will share with you my "Signature Roadmap of Scaling" called the SCALEit Method®, through which I outline how you can multiply your growth across a variety of assets, including: retaining and recruiting the best talent; creating a collaborative, efficient, and satisfying workplace environment; developing new products and services and/or building your core customer base; and producing an ever-flowing stream of cash flow with consistent profits. In addition, I show how you can build a business that has deeper meaning for you – and one that can impact the world in a positive way.

Let me emphasize one crucial point: *Doubling your business does not mean working doubly hard with your sweat equity.* Instead, it is about leveraging your team's talents and your own intellectual and leadership capital to successfully apply one or more of the sixteen scalable strategies presented. Visual tools, checklists, and spreadsheets illustrate these discussions and, as a bonus, you will find them continually updated on the following website: www. ScaleorFail.com/bonus.

The Five Components of SCALE

There are five components that are central in scaling your company. Each of these five levels of the SCALEit Method are described with exact steps to follow and are highlighted with powerful stories of the amazing clients I have had the honor to know and work with over the years.

   S: Strategic Vision: Knowing where you are headed is crucial in order to figure out how to get there. Yet most business owners don't have a clear destination in mind and, as you might imagine, this is a big reason why they flail about instead of remaining steadily on course. Your Strategic Vision – or "Big Picture Vision," as I call it – is your personal Yellow Brick Road to the Emerald City. It is the inspiration that keeps you determined and moving forward, regardless of the obligatory rejections and brick walls you will face. Creating the right Big Picture Vision is the key to being able to successfully scale your business.

   C: Cash Flow: Think of cash flow as the life force of your company. It ensures you are breathing and pumping blood to the core systems of your business so they will thrive and grow. You must build a revenue-driven business that creates cash for your business on a daily basis. Applying the cash flow practices discussed in the book will give you the vitals you need to invest in your Big Picture Vision.

A: **Alliance of the Team:** You, as the leader, are the Visionary. It is up to you to attract and surround yourself with creative talent and how-to experts who can transform your vision into reality. That includes your taking the lead to build a culture that aligns your team with your Big Picture Vision and feeds off your passion and energy.

L: **Leadership:** Guiding your team on your Big Picture Vision journey means you must become the best possible version of yourself. If you want to expand your business by 50%, then you must grow personally by at least *60%* to be able to attain that station, carry the weight, and then have the emotional, physical, and intellectual reserves to lead it. Your own personal growth fuels the courage necessary to lead this mission.

E: **Execution:** Action is where all of your magic comes to life. Action is where you apply and perfect your Big Picture Vision so you can leap higher and higher in both profits and impact. Action, not perfection, is the true measure of how well you executed your best-laid plans. Contrary to what most entrepreneurs believe, miscalculations, mistakes, and course corrections are among the best assets in your business. *Failures* are never really failures; they are doorways into much better things, if you react properly to them.

In building 10 companies – 4 of which I sold – I know the high-highs and the low-lows oh so well. I have weathered many breakdowns and dead-ends on my way to the breakthroughs and the big wins. I would not trade one moment of those experiences – even the painful ones – because so many of my smartest pivots came from my darkest times.

Here's the deal. To get out of nowhere land, you must upsize your strategic practices, implement new marketing strategies, find new ways to build your team, and expand your mindset to break through whatever is keeping you stuck at the same level. You must believe in the deepest part of your being that you can build your enterprise, regardless of whether or not you know exactly how to get there at this moment. Then you must be willing to take the leap into the giant unknown – to make your impossible possible.

Yes, it is a risk. But isn't anything you truly want worth such a risk? If your answer is *no* – if you are too afraid, too shy, or too this or too that – the alternative is that the dream you carry in your head will never become realized. To me, that is the saddest story of all.

So ask yourself: *Which is really the greater risk – going for it or living with the regret of not having gone for it for the rest of your life?*

Besides, there is no guarantee the status quo will remain the status quo. Things change. Markets change. *You* change. If you think sitting tight will "keep you safe," I suggest you spend some time thinking that through. If you don't make the commitment to build a new structure for your company, one of three things will most likely happen:

1. You will squander opportunities to leap from entrepreneur to enterprise.
2. You will be a sinkhole in your own growth and maybe even get swallowed by it.
3. You will find your company disrupted by the latest innovation that you didn't see coming.

I don't want to see any of this happen to you – and it does not need to. All *can'ts* must be tossed out the window. You *can* achieve your dreams – *and you will*.

Who I Am – And Why I Believe I Can Help You

I am so grateful that I found my calling early on as a business owner at age 19. Now, in what seems like a lifetime later, I have the opportunity to help business owners like you turn your small business ventures into enterprises. I am rewarded when I see entrepreneurs bestow their greatest works upon the world.

For over a dozen years, as the CEO of Allison Maslan International, I have been blessed to coach thousands of business owners from their infancy to achieving revenue streams of eight and nine figures. In 2010, I founded Pinnacle Global Network, Business Mentoring and Mastermind, which is a world leader in business advising and mentoring. We guide established business owners to grow and scale solid companies – many of whom ultimately double and triple their revenue in less than one year.

The Power Is Right at Your Fingertips

Scaling a business, like performing on a trapeze, requires a balance of will and skill. You become an expert at learning the right steps, tools, and principles – the central principal being that it all starts with you as the business owner, founder, and CEO. Everything starts with your decisions and actions. I commend you for all of the accomplishments that have led you to this place.

Business is definitely not for the faint of heart. Many give up before they even reach this point. I'm sure you've had many moments of doubt – we all have! But your tenacity and spirit have gotten you *here*. Now, it's time for you to develop the structure, systems, roadmap, and mindset you need to get *there*.

Whether your ultimate desire is to sell your company for a three- to five-time evaluation, run it for the next several years for continued cash flow and personal fulfillment, or pass it down to your family and to future generations, *Scale or Fail* offers you an ideal roadmap to success. You and your executive team may refer to it time and again as a company bible of sorts every time you need a refresher course on what to do when the business flattens out.

I encourage you to approach *Scale or Fail* from a new perspective – with fresh eyes and a new vision of *what can be*. Once you let go of what is no longer working and holding your organization back, you will be able to enter into a whole new world of remarkable opportunities.

Thank you for giving me the opportunity to support you on your next big journey. Let the adventure begin!

1

It All Starts with the First Leap

Leap and the net will appear.

—John Burroughs, naturalist and essayist

My Story

One morning 20 years ago, I woke up feeling buried by my business. No matter how hard I worked, I could not relieve what felt like a 1,000-pound weight on my shoulders: constant work, unrelenting chores, never-ending bills, and round-the-clock parental responsibilities raising my 2-year-old daughter, Gabriella, by myself. I was running on empty with no time or energy to do the activities I liked or be with the people who brought me joy. In fact, I had lost the motivation to seek out joy because all I could think about was the oppressive stress that was running my life – wondering how I was going to get everything done before collapsing after midnight, only to start the cycle all over again the next day. To top it off, I was constantly wracked with the guilty feeling that I was a horrible parent. Ironically, I had started this business to become the master of my fate – to live a life of freedom and creativity and build a wonderful life for my daughter.

At the time, I was running my company, The Barali Group, a full-service advertising and public relations firm in San Diego, California. Business was good – no, it was better than good, it was shooting through the roof. I was being slammed with business from Fortune 100 companies such as Ben & Jerry's, Supercuts, Allstate, and Charlotte Russe. The cash was flooding in. I should have been counting my blessings, right? My ship had come in. Unfortunately, this was not at all the case. I had no time to breathe, much less any free time to spend all of the money I was earning.

What was going on? Was I just being ungrateful for my good fortune?

I tried to sort out the problem, as something was dreadfully wrong. While the front end of my business was booming, the back end – the glue that held everything together – was nonexistent.

For one thing, I had a small, talented team, but needed to face the fact that I was naïve and ill-prepared to lead them. Rather than delegate tasks to my staff to free myself up and live my life, I continued to be involved in every aspect of – well, *everything*! I performed an honest self-diagnosis and came to the conclusion that I was a total control freak. (As I later discovered, this is a universal trait among people who start their own businesses from scratch.)

Meanwhile, I was a control freak who didn't have anything resembling a blueprint for growth and, of course, no plan in place to scale and adapt to all of the changes occurring in my business. Although I was a whiz at bringing in clients and had a knack for building successful ad campaigns, I was sorely lacking the ability to manage anything beyond that and unable to concede enough authority to empower anyone on my staff to rise to the occasion and fill in the gaps. We haphazardly bounced from one project to the next. My team and I suffered many all-nighters loaded up on coffee in order to meet crazy deadlines. We were all breathing our own exhaust.

My Big Wake-up Call

Most of us can look back on our lives and recognize the wake-up call that set the course for our future. The moment when our lives took a drastic turn and the universe tossed us out on our derrieres, forcing us to make a change – whether we were ready for it or not. In most instances, we were not.

When you are under constant stress, one of the side effects is that you are never living in the moment. You are constantly trying to figure out what you need to do next, rather than paying attention to the brilliant opportunities for joy and prosperity right in front of you. You fail to see or feel the vision, as you are focusing so much on your day-to-day workload, your frustrations, and your own *stuckness*. (Yes, I admit I just made up that word, since that is the best way to describe the sensations involved.)

My wake-up call occurred on the day when I managed to run over myself with my own car. Yes, you read that correctly: *I ran over myself with my own car.* This feat was clearly the biggest faux pas of my life.

It happened when I was picking Gabriella up at daycare. I was in a rush from another long workday – running late, as always – and parked my Ford Taurus in haste. I began my leap out of the vehicle in a panic, feeling the shame of being tardy to pick up my child and exhaustion from hours of toiling nonstop at the office. I'm sure you can guess what happened as I exited the car.

Surprise! I realized too late that I had failed to use the parking brake. As the car began to move with me in its grip, halfway out of the driver's seat, it dawned on me that my frenetic pace was doing me in.

The car rolled back, dragging me underneath the front tire and out into the middle of the street. If having a 4,000-pound car running over you does not cause you to drastically reexamine everything about your life, nothing will. Once the car stopped rolling, I realized that it was only by some incredible miracle that I had survived in one piece (except for the tire tracks on my legs, which lasted for a year). I knew my life had to change.

The following question popped into my head loud and clear: *Do you want to be in the same place a year from now, and 10 years from now?*

The thought of living like this for another year – much less another day – lit a raging fire under my feet. I made a drastic decision and walked away from everything. I essentially handed my half of the business to my partner, left my failing marriage, and rebooted. I went back out into the world as a single mom with no money, no revenue, no prospects, and no idea what I was going to do with my life.

The result? I was happier than I had been in years.

From that point onward, I made a decision that I must be 100% passionate about everything I did – or else I would drop it. The choice was either "Hell yes!" or "No way!" There wasn't anything in between. I loved the idea of business and making money, but I arrived at the conclusion that there had to be a better way than riding myself so hard that I ended up literally running over myself.

My Business Blueprints Are Born

I spent the entire following year rebuilding my life. I made a list of all the parts of my company that worked well and separated out which ones were broken, faulty, or missing altogether. Next I dove into each individual aspect to figure out why some things worked while others didn't. I also studied my clients who ran successful companies, examining the systems and processes that had turned them into well-oiled machines functioning with fluid perfection and garnering sustainable results over both the short and long term.

> Every successful business owner has that pivotal moment in their lives and careers. I call mine "the moment of impact."
>
> Mine happened to occur during a "wonderful thing" called the Recession. It was a terrible time for everyone. All of my eggs were in one basket with retailers. But I was afraid to go to them and continue to do business. Buyers I had worked with for years had lost their jobs, and I was worried. Stores were shuttering. Companies had filed for bankruptcy.
>
> I had spent so much time and energy pleasing my buyers, doing things like sending them cupcakes. But my company wasn't going to survive this way. The Recession taught me that I no longer needed to worry about my buyers. I needed to worry about my customers.

My focus completely changed. My business started going direct to consumer. We weren't going to worry about our wholesalers and retail partners anymore. Of course, we still did business with them when there were opportunities – but mostly I redirected everything to customers.

I had only seven employees at the time. I maxed out my credit card and line of credit. I pulled out of the rep groups and opened my own showrooms. I built a direct-to-consumer website. I created the "color bar" where the customer could design her own jewelry; she'd pick the colors she wanted and choose her own metals.

We did the unthinkable and opened our first retail store. It was a calculated risk during the Recession. But retailers were shuttering, so space was cheap and I was able to negotiate my own great lease.

Everyone thought I was out of my mind. While everyone else was pulling out, I was trying to do something disruptive, innovative, and creative.

I wasn't going to allow anyone to speak for me again. I was going to build my own relationships with customers to find out for myself what they loved and hated. And that's when the magic started.

Years later: I now have a $1 billion business and 2,000 employees – all due to that moment of impact.

—Excerpt from my interview with Kendra Scott, chairman, CEO, and lead designer of Kendra Scott, LLC. To watch my full interview with Kendra Scott, go to: www.ScaleorFail.com/bonus.

From all of this, I developed two strategic blueprints: one to *grow* a business and the other to *scale* a business. I diagrammed these blueprints like an architect renders drawings for the construction of a new building. I subsequently adhered to them step-by-step as I built nine more companies – four of which of I've sold – that have generated tens of millions of dollars.

Most important, I had a blast along the way. I finally *enjoyed* what I was doing, while at the same time accomplishing my goals and making lots of money. No longer was I breathing my own exhaust fumes. I created businesses that improved my quality of life, allowing me to spend time with my family and friends and even savor my two passions: travel and flying on the trapeze.

Over these past three decades, I have carried wisdom from one business to the next and from one client to the next. I have since refined both blueprints so that the principles can be replicated and adapted, regardless of the industry or business model. Whether you run a brick-and-mortar storefront or an online business, the SCALEit Method® enables you to scale while working on your personal growth and development as a true CEO, instead of being a worker bee running every detail of an organization that is actually spinning you around in circles. The SCALEit Method is adaptable to any type of business – manufacturing, consumer goods, a brick-and-mortar store, a digital service, a wholesaler, a consulting service, and everything in between.

I share my story and use it to illustrate my philosophy of scaling because I discovered through working with my clients that what I had experienced as a small business owner was not unique. The clients I work with all have their own versions of feeling trapped inside their businesses. They are lost in their own self-created mazes of never-ending tasks, responsibilities, options, decisions, and ups and downs – and they have no clue how to extricate themselves from the day-to-day minutiae and focus on the bigger picture.

I see this prevailing issue festering in start-ups, $20 million businesses, and even companies nearing or exceeding $100 million: the leaders fear that their businesses will fall apart if they quit being the worker bees and stop overseeing and approving every single detail. Some of them secretly worry they don't know anything other than what they are doing and hold on tight to performing the work activities they have done well for years rather than confront the unknown and fail. As a result, they run around in their company's maze, often ending up right back where they started. Each day is a painful repeat of the day before with no end in sight, and the company remains lodged in second gear. It's time to cue up the classic film about déjà vu, *Groundhog Day*, and its daily repeat of Sonny and Cher's "I Got You Babe" on the radio! With the right direction, blueprint, and courage to implement, you can achieve the success you desire and finally move on to February 3 (the day after Groundhog Day). Fear not: I will show you how.

The Power of Failure

In most cases, failure does not come from taking the leap. It comes from giving up before you've given yourself a chance to step up the ladder to the platform and soar. You look up and panic before you even arrive there.

Your mind races to the negative possibilities: *What if I fail and fall? What if I get into debt and can't pay my bills?* You hear all of the naysaying voices in your head: your spouse, your mother, your father, your best friends, your cousins, your former colleagues, and even acquaintances who know little about you. They even gave you the added bonus of telling you each and every business horror story and failure they ever heard. Sometimes they just innocently ask, "Are you sure you are ready for this?"

Even if they have the best of intentions, it's as if they are all hoping you'll fail – just to be able to say those fatal words: *I told you so.*

I love this statement, often attributed to motivational speaker T. Harv Eker: "Every master was once a disaster." Sometimes you must crash into the wall, hit rock bottom, or, like me, run over yourself to realize you must find another direction.

Fortunately, my personal disaster was not the end of my story. It actually marked the beginning.

I became hell-bent on discovering an alternate way to build a successful business and create a meaningful life that would bring happiness to the ones I loved as well as to myself. Failure gifted me with a breakthrough like no other life experience.

Failure gives you the insight to look at your experiences in a new light. Yes, these moments can be excruciatingly painful, and we obviously don't go looking for failure. But that is exactly where the growth happens. When everything is copacetic and operating smoothly, there is nothing compelling you to look within and examine the deeper questions that provide you with opportunities to make the biggest shifts in your life.

Without these crucial phases, business owners may stay stuck in second gear – the state in which you are floating in a static mode, where there's no electric charge or potential for any new energy or movement. You're idling in mid-air or in a black hole, feeling stuck, trapped, frustrated, and confused about what action or direction to take to propel yourself forward. Then, *boom*, you hit the proverbial wall and are ready for your wake-up call.

Failure is a teacher who gives lessons that you will never forget. It's what you do with this education that counts. This one changed my life for the better, and I am forever grateful.

What's the Meaning Behind the Money?

In tearing my ad agency apart bit by bit, I was able to identify where the gaps were, what parts of the foundation were weak, and why I could not seem to get ahead – no matter how hard I tried. The biggest hole was loss of passion. I had thought the most important part of growing a business was making lots of money. I was wrong.

Don't misunderstand me: It goes without saying that you need to create revenue and profits to scale your company. Money has the power to transform lives, and I want to help you create great wealth in your business – inside and out. Money is essential to invest in your growth, and it helps you support those you care about. There is also your team and their families to consider. Their financial survival and success depends entirely on yours.

> If it's only about the money, you are going to give up. Having a "cool idea" and "making lots of money" are not good enough. You have to have something inside you, a calling, a purpose. That will fuel you at 3:00 a.m. when other people are giving up.
> —*Excerpt from a recent interview with PeterDiamandis, founder of the X Prize Foundation. To watch the full interview, go to: www.ScaleorFail.com/bonus.*

The challenge comes when money is your *sole motivator.* That was the problem I experienced with my advertising agency. The bank account was filling up with cash, but my heart remained empty. In fact, it was bleeding out. I had believed that money was the answer yet, at the end of the day, it's not what is most fulfilling or what drives you on the path toward achieving wealth. It's the work, the people, and the experiences along the way that give purpose and meaning to what you are doing.

I longed for more meaningful relationships with my clients and a sense of purpose. I wanted to know that my team and I were making a difference. I wanted my company to have a lasting and positive impact on others. I felt we were only as good as our last campaign and not being uplifted by the experience. With my newfound outlook, I was able to truly enjoy our clients. In fact, I have now worked with many clients for a long time and count them among my friends.

Trust me when I stress that at best money is only half the equation (albeit a critical half). It powers your business engine to rotate the flywheel. Money can make it go faster and faster. But without one essential ingredient, your flywheel will spin out of control and become irreparably broken.

Passion Brings the Cash In

In order for an activity or goal to sustain itself long enough to be successful through life's inevitable ups and downs, there must be meaning and passion behind it. It is imperative that you love what you do. Passion is what enables you to cherish your wins and lifts you right back on your feet when you face setbacks and losses. Without passion, business becomes a grind, a job. When an activity or goal has meaning for you, you're more likely to give your heart and soul to this cause, making sure that you stay focused, labor over every detail, and absorb yourself in every moment. When you spend time on efforts that really matter to you, it's far more likely that you'll make the commitment that's necessary in order to build an entity capable of sustaining, thriving, and scaling.

> Passion is energy. Feel the power that comes from focusing on what excites you.
>
> —*Oprah Winfrey*

In having studied many successful companies and interviewed founders who continue to thrive in their companies, I have found that they all have this in common: *They love their business.* They love what it stands for, the people in it, and the impact they are making. They rise above the chaos, they grow through the ups and downs, and they revel in the wins. They are in total alignment with the company vision and everything the company stands for. Their passion is contagious and translates outward to their employees, customers, and partners. People seek to work for these companies because they want to experience this passion firsthand.

Ask yourself the following questions:

1. Do you love your business?
2. Is your passion visible to your team?

3. Do your team members seem passionate about what they do?
4. Does the shared passion provide staff members with the opportunity to shine?
5. Do you have core company values?
6. Are your company values shared with the team?

Now that you have taken that first scary leap, have accepted that it's okay to fail, have identified your passion, and have welcomed your team along to share in your vision, it's time to begin strategizing.

Chapter Summary: You've Got This!

- DON'T wait for your wake-up call to start converting your business into an enterprise.
- DON'T let yourself get trapped inside your own business.
- DON'T be afraid of failure. It's okay to fail!
- DON'T let money be your sole purpose.
- DO be passionate about what you do.
- DO transmit the passion and energy to your team.
- DO take your first leap to scale!

2

Your Strategic Vision

Throw your heart over the bars and your body will follow.
—Anonymous trapeze artist

My Final Lesson from My Father

My father built and ran several innovative women's clothing chains for many years. Stewarts and Extension One were based in the midwestern states; Irma Dumas was in Arkansas; Mademoiselle was in Memphis; and Worth's was in West Virginia. At one time his enterprise was the largest privately owned women's ready-to-wear chain in the United States, with over 50 locations. He was incredibly passionate about this business, which consumed his life.

Over time, he had big successes – and suffered major losses, too. He learned to maneuver his way through all of the ups and the downs. During my last visit with him, just before he left this Earth a few years ago, he was still talking business. That had always been his language of choice and where we, as father and daughter, intersected the most.

I held his hand as he lay in bed staring at the ceiling. He proceeded to tell me that his business had been rewarding to him.

When I asked him what was the most rewarding part about his work, his reply took me by surprise: "Helping people."

His answer perplexed me. As I mentioned, my dad sold women's fashions. He wasn't a doctor, health-care worker, social worker, firefighter, or police officer. How was he "helping people"? Did he believe he had enabled women to look better and feel better about themselves through the clothing in his stories? Did he believe he'd helped his thousands of employees by giving them a nice place to work and steady income?

I had to know for sure and asked, "Helping them *what*, Dad?"

He paused and replied, "Helping people have the momentum to move forward in their lives." In that instant, he had taken my breath away. He had told me his underlying *Why* – what had driven him to keep going through all the highs and lows.

What a gift he had given me. This was a revelation!

I always knew that I learned business from my dad, but I wasn't sure where I had acquired that deep desire to help people move past their obstacles and create success. With this one statement shared from his heart, everything suddenly made sense to me.

Not only did I now understand where my intense – sometimes over the top – drive had come from, I now had clarity about my *Why*.

Your Strategic Vision Starts with a Dream

Dreamers see beyond boundaries and limits. They question the validity of everything. They see hope and abundance where others see walls and impossibilities.

I work on my mindset toward achieving my dream every single day. In order to expand your business another 40%, you must grow as a CEO by 60% so you can sustain that growth. To bust out of the norm and create a revolutionary vision for your company, you must exercise your brain and your guts on a daily basis.

> This is the life that I've chosen to lead. I feel like I've been gifted this life, that I have to do something that actually helps people. I share with people a lot – especially entrepreneurs – [and I believe that] we all have this choice while we're here on this planet.
>
> —*Excerpt from my interview with Kara Goldin, CEO and founder of Hint Inc. For the full interview, go to: www.ScaleorFail.com/bonus.*

With the above in mind, I will explain how to design your Strategic Vision – which I also call the Big Picture Vision.

I cannot overemphasize the power and importance of creating the perfect Strategic Vision. It marks the beginning of your SCALEit Method Blueprint and serves as your roadmap for *Why* you do the things you do as CEO of your company. It also helps determine *Where* you are headed and *How* you will get there.

> Every business has a story to tell.
> —*Jay Baer, business strategist and keynote speaker*

The SCALEit Method in Motion

The SCALEit Method starts with Strategic Vision (this chapter), then moves to Cash Flow (Chapter 3), Alliance of the Team (Chapter 4), Leadership (Chapter 5), and Execution (Chapter 6), where everything comes together. Use the chart in Figure 2.1 to write out the top three suggestions in each phase of the SCALEit Method that you connect with most and want to execute.

Your Big Picture Vision

Your Big Picture Vision is what drives you to keep pushing forward to make your dream a reality, no matter what circumstances arise. This represents what values your company truly stands for, the deeper meaning behind it, how you should best express your products and/or services in the marketplace, and where you intend to lead your company in the future.

Your Big Picture Vision tells the story of your business. The cast is made up of you and your team. The audience consists of your customers, partners, fans, and prospects.

PINNACLE GLOBAL NETWORK®
THE WORLD LEADER IN SCALING BUSINESSES

The **SCALEit Method**®

Write three strategies in each area that you are committing to implement.

STRATEGIC PLAN

completion date

1.
2.
3.

CASH FLOW

completion date

1.
2.
3.

ALLIANCE OF THE TEAM

completion date

1.
2.
3.

LEADING THE WAY

completion date

1.
2.
3.

EXECUTION OF THE PLAN

completion date

1.
2.
3.

© Allison Maslan International

Figure 2.1: The SCALEit Method leads to unimaginable success.

As with every good story, you need to create a strong plot to keep the cast and the audience engaged throughout the process and vested in the outcome.

The key with your Big Picture Vision is to go all out with it – no holds barred. It allows you to break through the ceiling that keeps you small. It enables you to welcome your team into the process and becomes a wonderful bonding exercise, as you will see. The ideas and solutions you originate out of thin air have the capacity to create millions – perhaps even *billions* – in wealth, as well as happiness and peace of mind. Now *that* is a dream worth chasing!

Stop Chasing Emergencies

It shouldn't be surprising that so many CEOs and their companies lose their way toward chasing their dreams. They started off in business with a real connection to the *why* and *what* they sought to create. The leaders were inspired from deep inside their core, hyped-up, and ready to conquer the world.

As the years went by and companies went down their respective paths, they morphed due to a range of factors – developments in their industries, changes in the economy, the results of their business decisions, the demands of clients, the quality of their products and services, and so on. Without even realizing what was happening, business owners gradually shifted their roles from being drivers to being passengers. The dreams that had started it all faded over time.

Is this the case for you and your business? Instead of leading your Big Picture Vision, are you constantly putting out fires, scrambling to meet deadlines, struggling to meet payroll, managing cash flow, and battling for industry market share and customer mindshare? If you only had one more day in the week you'd be able to get it all done, right? *Absolutely not.* As I've discovered, business owners always manage to wrap back around to handling the fires, the deadlines, the payrolls, the cash flow, and their share of the market. Business owners have an uncanny knack for filling each day with unnecessary tasks – or at least ones that could be delegated to a more appropriate staff member.

> **Alice:** Would you tell me, please, which way I ought to go from here?
> **Cheshire Cat:** That depends a good deal on where you want to get to.
> —*from* Alice in Wonderland, *by Lewis Carroll*

If you are like these business owners, how does this approach bring you any closer to attaining your dreams? It doesn't. Sure, you might be squeaking by and paying bills and salaries but, as time passes, you become so buried in repairing screw-ups and responding to everyone's demands, expectations, and fears that you become overwhelmed. Your *why* has become that faded dream from a distant past.

Your team sees you only as a firefighter – not as a leader. Rather than focusing on what is important – continuous personal and professional growth and fulfillment of your passion – you are constantly chasing the emergencies, which is the kiss of death in business. Instead of moving forward, you are running around in circles – which means no growth and merely surviving, not thriving.

> Everything is impossible until someone does it. If someone is going to do it, why can't it be you?
> The reality is this: It's critical for you to connect with, and have great passion for, whatever it is that you do. The most important thing is your mission, your purpose – or, as I call it, your "massively transformative purpose."
> —*Excerpt from a recent interview with PeterDiamandis, founder of the XPrize Foundation. To watch the full interview, go to: www.ScaleorFail.com/bonus.*

You are most likely thinking: "Yes, I get that my Vision and Mission are crucial. However, right now I just need to focus on getting this project done or I'll lose this customer."

The irony is that most CEOs and their teams have become so disconnected from their visions that, if they were to have the courage to step back and re-embrace it, most of their emergencies would never have even surfaced. There wouldn't be such great risk of losing that customer. Creating a Strategic Vision and relentlessly sticking to it inherently prevents all types of issues, including those related to your customers, your team, and your cash flow. I initially wrote about how to create your Big Picture Vision in my first book, *Blast Off!: The Surefire Success Plan to Launch Your Dreams in Reality*. Why? Because it works. Creating a story and intention of what you want your life or business to look like is like writing an order to the Universe. Now you just need to back it up with relentless action.

When my client, Liz Papagni, was growing her company, Marketing Initiative Worx, she was in the sweet spot of her vision and talents assisting big brands such as Seneca Foods and Kern's Nectar with the launches of their food products. As overhead began to grow, as is the case for many new businesses, she began taking on clients that were too small and did not fit in with her Big Picture Vision. They may have helped with immediate cash flow, but slowed her growth toward greater capacity. Her Pinnacle Business Mentor and I worked together on revamping her entire scale strategy. Once she saw the potential for multiplying her profits by letting those smaller projects go and focusing on the whales, she was able to confidently and successfully get back on track toward her Big Picture Vision.

Your passion is a central tenet toward achieving success and your Strategic Vision is the bridge that transports that passion into a sustained future. Let's reconnect with your passion and start building your bridge.

It takes courage to think bigger than you normally do. It isn't easy mapping out your dream world one year from now, much less five years from now. Doing so provides you with the confidence you always had buried in yourself with regard to what you have to offer to the world. Creating your Big Picture Vision not only convinces you that what you had thought was impossible is indeed possible, it reconfigures your brain patterns away from a fear-based strategy toward where your passion is driving you to go.

For those of you who are golf lovers, think of it this way: "The Bear Trap" at the PGA National Champion Golf Course starting at the 15th hole is known as one of the most demanding three-hole stretches in the world. It was designed with water on the right and a sand trap on the left. The pin is only 150 yards away. Many pros choke in their effort to avoid the water and end up pulling the ball to the left and landing it in the sand trap. The best strategy, in golf or business, is to keep your eye on the big vision and play to win, rather than play not to lose.

In business, when you get sucked into the anticipation of not making payroll or the minutia of the details, you risk losing your vision, making fear-based decisions, and sabotaging your success. Keep your eye on the prize, apply the SCALEit Method along the way, and the *how* will fall into place to get you there.

Big Picture Vision Exercise

Let's see where you stand with your vision by trying out an exercise. You'll need to take some time away from distractions for a few hours so you can think clearly and get creative. Find a place where you are comfortable and relaxed and can clear your mind. I happen to live in San Diego, so I love to go sit in the sand at the beach. Choose your own setting and free yourself from distractions (i.e., turn your phone off – you can do it!). All you need to bring is a photocopy of the bulleted list that follows, a photocopy of the Big Picture Vision Mind Map (Figure 2.2), a pad of paper, and a couple of pens.

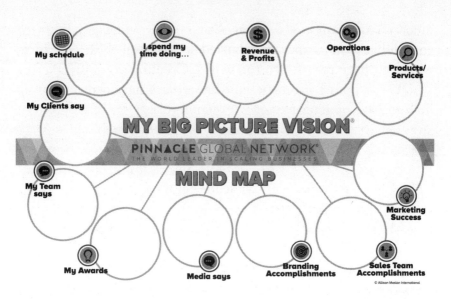

Figure 2.2: The Big Picture Vision Mind Map gives you an idea of what your future can look like.

Once you are situated and relaxed, free your mind and begin to answer the following questions quickly, as soon as the answer comes to you. Do not overthink the questions and do not edit your answers. Allow the words to flow directly from your mind onto the page. You want to tap deep within your "higher self" to get a true read on where you want to be five years from now in your business. What comes up in your mind when you imagine your company's growth five years into the future?

Let's break down each aspect of this mental picture to get crystal clear on your five-year vision. Answer the following questions directly inside your Big Picture Vision Mind Map. It is critically important that you do not worry about the *how* because any analyzing will stop your creative flow. The *how* will unfold over time, so let it go for this process. Write your answers in present tense, as if five years into the future is happening now.

- What are your daily and weekly schedules like?
- How are you spending your time?

- What is your current revenue?
- What do the operations of your company look like? How are they run?
- What added products and/or services have you produced and are now monetizing?
- What are you achieving with your marketing?
- What does the sales department of your company consist of?
- What has your branding accomplished?
- What is the media saying about you?
- What are you being recognized for? (Examples: awards, recognition, etc.)
- What does your team say about you?
- What are your clients saying about you?

You want to make sure you have a strong sense of your personal mission. What is that pain that you experienced in the past that you do not want others to experience? If you can take that mission and tie it to your goal, you will always want to go big. That pain will drive you forward.

—*Excerpt from a recent interview with Vishen Lakhiani, CEO, MindValley. To see the full interview, go to: www.ScaleorFail.com/bonus.*

Once you have finished filling out the Big Picture Mind Map, take the notes in the circles and write a complete story about this vision on your notepad. If you were living that vision now, what would that experience be like for yourself? What would it look like to the outside world? What would it feel like to be running this company? Write down every aspect of the vision that you want to create. The more detailed you are, the better. Refine the story until it feels right.

This is the Big Picture Vision of your business – what you intend to create. Now it is time to start visualizing this new vision into your current reality.

The Triple-It Factor

Now let's take your Big Picture Vision a step (or three steps) further. When I ask my clients to think big, there is a natural inclination to stretch themselves a little – maybe 10% or even 30%. For most people, if you have not experienced reaching massive goals it's challenging to stretch your imagination beyond your current reality. If you try to, all of those old self-doubts emerge to the surface whispering (or screaming) disempowering thoughts, such as: "I could never do that," "I feel like a phony," or "Who do I think I am to ever accomplish that?"

The following exercise is one of my favorites and helps people bust through those limiting thoughts and think bigger than ever before.

Close your eyes. Take a big deep breath and, for a moment, let go of anything that you are worrying about or distracted by. Now imagine the absolute biggest vision for your business and life that you can possibly see in your mind's eye. What is a massive change you want to bring about in the world? What do you love? What pisses you off? How do you see your business changing lives? Is it going global, revolutionizing your industry, creating a viral brand, or franchising your concept worldwide? Whatever it is, forget about the *how* and allow yourself to dream in magnanimous proportions. Hold that vision in your mind. What does it look like? How would it feel to be living that dream right now? How will others feel about the results of your vision? Okay ... are you ready? Here is the kicker. Now I want you to *triple* your dream. Yes, your blockbuster dream is now three times the size of your initial expanded thinking. For most people, this process takes their breath way because they have never allowed themselves to dream in such a colossal way. This, my friends, is the experience of thinking big. First you have to see it and believe it, and then you can make it real.

Visualization: See It. Feel It. Do It.

Visualization isn't magic, though sometimes it might seem like it is. There is a great deal of science behind it. Dr. Robin S. Vealey, author of *Coaching for the Inner Edge*, believes that when we rehearse a performance in our imagination, our muscles respond in a way that simulates the actual activity. It's as if a mental roadmap is being created to prepare us for the real thing. That's why athletes visualize their moves over and over again until their plans become emblazoned in their physical memories.

I have always used visualization in my business and in my personal life. Each time before I take my leap off the trapeze, I visualize my flight and the mid-air trick I am about to execute. I see myself spinning or floating around, whatever that particular trick might involve. I see and feel myself taking the leap, gaining height, spinning in the air, and then being caught by the catcher. Once I see it in my mind, I gain clarity in my body. The two go together well! Having clarity in the body creates confidence, and confidence is a key to success.

Everything you can imagine is real.

—*Pablo Picasso, artist*

Think Visual!

While you are sitting in your quiet space, review the answers you wrote on your notepad with your scribbles in the circles on the Big Picture Vision Mind Map. Update your Big Picture Vision now that you have done the Triple-It Factor Exercise.

How far are you from where you would like to be in five years? It may seem like light years – but that's okay! Your future begins right now.

Read over everything you wrote: where you would like to see yourself and your company in five years; the people around you; the size and makeup of your team; the innovative products and/or services you are selling; the new customer base you have formed; what you are doing with all of the free time you have; the company's illustrious reputation; the areas where you dominate; the awards you've won; the piles of revenue your company brings in; and the excess profit you are enjoying.

> When you visualize, then you materialize.
> —*Denis Waitley, motivational speaker and consultant*

Now that you have read over what you've written, surrender to it and accept it all as 100% fact. Close your eyes and believe with your heart, soul, and mind that this is your reality. Picture what everything looks like up close with clarity and in full color. Actually feel yourself in the present moment as if that vision is a reality … as if you are there right now experiencing the growth and results of your work. Repeat this visualization on a daily basis (morning and night) so it becomes ingrained in your unconscious mind.

Do you feel pumped about how you feel? You should! You have taken the first step toward making that mid-air jump. Congratulate yourself on your bravery. When you replay your vision like a movie – with you as the main character – right before you fall asleep every night, the images embed themselves in your subconscious mind. That sleepy state right before you fall asleep and as you begin to awake is when the subconscious grabs hold of your vision.

When you wake up in the morning, guess what you should do? Visualize! You'll do this again in the evening. This may seem like a lot, but it isn't. Think of yourself as an athlete training for a major event: The more you visualize, the clearer the picture and the greater chance everything you do will feed into helping making that vision come to fruition. For further reading on creating your vision, read *Vivid Vision* by Cameron Herold.

Vision Tools

The aforementioned general visualization exercise is just one of the many tools I use with my clients. There are several other tools and techniques you can test out to creatively reinforce your Big Picture Vision for yourself, your team, and your clients, customers, and partners. The more ways you work at this, the more ingrained, powerful, and enduring it will become. In addition, many of these techniques spark engagement with the people in your work universe. They can be *fun* and spread a sense of shared ownership within and outside your organization.

Improv Your Way to Your Vision

In comedy improvisation, the audience calls out random ideas and words and the comedians must spontaneously collaborate to create a skit on the fly. The results are often hilarious, and just watching that level of creative, quick-thinking energy merge into a coherent and fluid performance can be absolutely magical.

Believe it not, you can apply improvisation into your business as well. Yes, business is *fun*! This is a great method to get your team to be "in the moment" in a super-charged, creative way, and it becomes a lasting memory for everyone involved. Not only does it ensure that your vision doesn't become a horse pill for everyone to swallow regardless of whether they agree with it, it helps employees to feel as if they were part of its creation. In turn, they become more vested in your organization and develop a deeper sense of long-term commitment to the business.

It's so simple to get started and no one should feel nervous about "performing" in front of his or her peers. When it comes to improv, often it's the "screw-up moments" and weird, unexpected activities that lead to the biggest laughs and takeaways.

When I lead a client's team through an improvisation, I might say to them: "Imagine you're walking into your company five years from now. What is the experience like? What do you see? What do you feel?"

There is no "right or wrong" answer. It's all intended to be spontaneous. It's a remarkable experience for CEOs to see what their staff thinks about the company's future. Perhaps someone on your team reveals a creative side that no one knew existed. Or, someone has even grander ideas than you do. That is perfectly all right! You may or may not be 100% in sync with those ideas, but you want to listen to them, acknowledge them, and encourage that kind of positive attitude. You want your employees to think big and feel confident that your company is capable of creating remarkable things.

Companies have a way of "operationalizing" everyone and everything. Your employees end up being forced to do the same things day in and day out – only with greater accuracy, faster, and cheaper wherever possible. This improv process gets them out of "perfectionism mode" and removes the burden of their being stuck in *how* these amazing things will get accomplished, so the ideas and unique solutions pop up spontaneously.

Isn't this so much better than sitting around a table in a conference room brainstorming? I've found most of those sessions end up stagnant and unproductive because everyone – especially the CEO – feels the need to shoot down ideas before they are even fully aired. I'm sure all of these sound familiar: "Oh, we tried that and it didn't work," "It's too expensive," "We don't have the resources for that," "That isn't what we do here," and so on. It's much easier to be critical and kill an idea in its infancy rather than to originate one and pitch it.

Improvisation is effective because there is no room for criticism or judgment. It all mixes together – the good ideas and the bad ones. For this reason, no one feels wounded or embarrassed expressing an idea. It's all part of the entertainment and excitement. The team becomes part of the momentum, and the vision starts to come alive for everyone involved.

Rearview Casting

To shake things up, try something a little different. Instead of forecasting and looking five years ahead, pretend you are looking in the rearview mirror and *seeing that it has already happened.* Or, pretend you are sitting on a mountaintop, and you look behind you to see that your vision has come true. Through this process, you are visualizing that it has been completed with a feeling of certainty. You are sealing it in your mind as something well within your grasp because you have visualized it as already having occurred.

Rearview Casting is a form of meditation that helps you create a degree of confidence and ownership that you have done the task. It enables you to revel in the wonderful feeling of delight that you have accomplished such a brilliant work of art with your business. When you feel that sense of pleasure, it gives you even more incentive and inspiration to continue.

Go ahead. Try it now. Close your eyes. Take a deep breath and clear your mind. Shake your arms and your hands to release any stress and unwanted energy. Pretend you have completed your Big Picture Vision and you are turning around and looking back at the rewarding journey you have completed – all the ups and downs and major breakthroughs – and you have come out the other side. You feel a sense of pride that you did it, regardless of all the roadblocks along the way. You see how it all came together beautifully in the end, as well as the positive impact it had on your team, their families, and your customers. You feel elated and calm at the same time: the former because you conquered your dream; and the latter because your confidence in yourself has grown dramatically. You feel a strong knowingness in your heart. You have let go of any and all worry, insecurity, or confusion. You were right all along to pursue your dream vigorously. Congratulations!

You can also try this meditation with your team, as it helps demonstrate their important contributions to the process. They don't just hear about it, they get to *see* and *feel* it. You will find that Rearview Casting can be a complete game-changer.

In the End, the Story Is Remembered

People learn through stories because our lives are essentially made up of one story after another. Chances are you remember stories from your childhood more so than you do specific lessons from school. It's estimated that only 10% of any lecture actually gets retained. We recall stories better than straight information because our minds can follow and relate to them, thanks to an emotional connection we make with them.

Yes, there are many ways to learn. But these days, with the never-ending flood of information coming at us day and night from 24/7 digital communication sources, it's easy to tune out someone who is talking at you. Stories, on the other hand, take us on a journey and we become part of them. That's why I love using storytelling as a creative method with my clients and with my own team.

Here are a few ways to create your Big Picture Vision through Storytelling:

1. Take your Big Picture Vision Mind Map and then write it in story form as if your team is watching it transpire.
2. Create a storyboard about your Big Picture Vision and have the team act it out for you in the manner they choose.
3. Create a video story about your Big Picture Vision and share the journey of it coming to life.

Storytelling can be used to jumpstart your vision. If the stories you create are visual and powerful, they will make a lasting impression on your team.

Take the Next Steps with Your Big Picture Vision

Whether you use one or all of these tools, the end result will ultimately become your vision roadmap and the lifeblood of your success. It will elevate your company as a whole and create momentum like you have never seen before.

George Lucas: A Man with a Vision

When George Lucas presented a certain script to the studios, no one wanted it. They said no one likes science fiction and that it was for children, not adults. He finally found a producer who would finance it, but even he admitted he didn't care for the story. He only agreed to it because he wanted Lucas to make other movies for him in the future.

Lucas has recounted that, from the beginning, everything was stacked against him. He agreed to a paltry budget and a 300% salary cut. During the filming, electronics and props broke with regularity, and the entire set was devastated by a rainstorm. Most of the cast believed the film stunk and would be a flop. In spite of many continuing obstacles and challenges – some created by Lucas's own determination to rigidly stick to his vision – the film was finally completed and hit the theaters (albeit late).

To say that *Star Wars* became a "phenomenon" would be a grotesque understatement. It was the biggest box office winner of its time, launched a $27 billion business, and led to numerous financially successful sequels and prequels.

Once your Big Picture Vision is complete, share it with your team in a companywide meeting. Give everyone time to read it and invite them to express what stands out most for them. Watch the excitement in their faces when they see that they are part of a much bigger journey. It is human nature for people to want to grow and evolve. This new vision will enable them to feel that there are new frontiers ahead. They will adopt a renewed sense of pride working on your team to help you make this a reality.

Some companies will include the Big Picture Vision in their newsletter on a regular basis. Many of my team members post our Big Picture Vision on the walls near their computers. This serves as a constant reminder of our purpose for both the good days and the challenging ones. It also makes it abundantly clear that everyone serves an important role in making it happen.

Share your vision with your customers, your vendors, your prospects, and your job applicants. Many companies are so proud of their vision that they post it front and center on their websites for all to see as a sales, marketing, and recruiting tool. Who wouldn't want to work for or with a company that has such a great vision?

The more people you share your vision with, the more opportunity your company has to grow. Over time, the word will spread and you will attract those who are aligned to come on board as devoted employees, clients, valuable connections, and even potential investors.

There may be others who are opposed to or critical of your vision – the nonbelievers or negative critics. This is a good sign. It means that you are onto something! Smile back at them because you know in your heart that you are on the right path. Not everyone is a fan of Harley Davidsons or the iPhone, but that has not stopped either one of these companies. In fact, it makes their fans revel in their rebelliousness and devotion even more. If you have naysaying employees, get them off the bus as soon as you can, as they will hold you back and can poison and discourage the rest of your team. You want to surround yourself only with those people who are supportive, positive, and uplifting. Not everyone will align with your Big Picture Vision, and that is okay. You will fail while trying to please them all, so don't even bother.

Remember: You are visualizing your Big Picture Vision every morning and night. However, as new problems surface during the course of the day – and they always do – pull out your vision again to remind yourself *why you have chosen this path* and *why it is so important to stay on it.* Read it aloud and visualize it happening at that moment. You'll feel a renewed sense of confidence and strength to find the solutions you need to succeed.

In business, you are always vulnerable. You put your brave self out there every single day. You have big dreams and goals and, when the wins happen, it's exalting. There are also those inevitable challenging days when we get mired in stress or fear, or we worry that something is not turning out exactly the way we had hoped.

Sometimes, things don't work. We set aggressive goals for bigger accounts and higher revenue – but miss. That's okay! As we learned in Chapter 1, failure is expected. It's a cliché, but true: You are in a marathon, not a sprint. Stay the course.

In the future – when you look back on all you have accomplished – I hope you can reflect like my father did at 84 years of age and identify the most rewarding part of your career as *helping people.* Whether you are scaling an insurance company, a tech company, a furniture chain, an online retail business, or anything else, you and your team are flying in tandem on a trapeze. You are giving them the inspiration and vision to soar along with you and accomplish true greatness. When you grab their hands or they grab yours in mid-air, you are helping each other create a spectacle. *Magic.*

Isn't that what your vision is really all about?

Chapter Summary: You've Got This!

- DON'T allow yourself to spend all of your time chasing emergencies.
- DO create your Big Picture Vision and visualize it daily.
- DO test out other visualization exercises: Improvisation, Rearview Casting, and Storytelling.
- DO collaborate with your team to engage them in the Big Picture Vision.
- DO share your Big Picture Vision with your clients, customers, partners – and everyone else.
- DON'T ever give up on your Big Picture Vision – setbacks and failures are *expected* along the way.

3

All Things Cash Flow

Wealth is the ability to fully experience life.
—Henry David Thoreau, essayist and philosopher

The Day My Cash Flow Stopped

The following took place in 2009, at around the time of the Great Recession. I vividly remember because I was running my homeopathic practice at the time and had several clients desperate to alleviate their fears of the looming economic catastrophe and the detrimental impact it was about to have on their lives. I listened supportively, but made sure not to engage with their fears because I understand the power of how we can sabotage a great business – or anything for that matter – by focusing on negative thoughts.

This time, the circumstances were getting harder to ignore. It seemed as if almost everyone I talked to was focusing on his or her intensified fear of the future and sense of becoming overwhelmed. I didn't think I was buying into their frenzy, but gradually I noticed that my phone had stopped ringing. No one was calling to make an appointment. This was odd, because I was always booked solid.

The few potential clients who did call asked my fees. After I told them they said, "Oh, I can't afford that." My fees had been the same for the past year, so something was clearly amiss.

The first week, I attributed it to the fact that I needed a break. After two more weeks went by, Julie, my assistant, asked, "Allison, what is going on?"

I replied, "I have no idea."

And then, I started to worry. In fact, I began to feel a great deal of fear rising up in my gut. Then I heard myself talking as I shared my worries with my husband. It was as if I were observing myself play out this fear. While all of this worry energy was bubbling over, it hit me like a sledgehammer: I had been falling – hook, line, and sinker – into my customers' stories.

No matter how hard I had been trying to distance myself, I was allowing their fears to seep into my thoughts. I was living out this belief that my abundance was coming to a screeching halt.

That day, I drove myself to the beach. I sat in the sand for what felt like hours. My goal was to shift my energy from a state of fear to reconnecting with my vision, passion, and place of abundance. I completed the visualization and once again experienced the joy of working with my clients and helping them heal. I visualized their happiness in my getting well, and how that would impact my clients' lives. I felt a powerful shift happening inside of me, moving from fear back to a place of abundance and gratitude.

You cannot feel fear and gratitude at the same time, so that helped me anchor my positive thoughts. I could feel the fear dissolve from my body and knew change was in store for my business and me.

The very next day, my phone rang nonstop. Julie called and exclaimed, "You did some visualization, didn't you!"

■ ■ ■

Cash flow is a crucial part of business and you must have rock-solid strategies in place to support your growth and protect you through the rocky times. However, before anything else, you first must believe it will all come together. There will always be down periods, but they won't stay that way as long as you remain focused on the vision of where you are going, believe it to your core, even if you are not there yet ... and then mix in a ridiculous amount of persistence.

If you truly believe in your mission, if you truly believe you want to make a difference on this planet, the money will be there. By getting into this place of worry and disbelief or non-belief, you're just pushing it away.

In my mind, cash flow is a living force. If you think of cash in terms of *currency*, it's not a big leap to regarding it as business energy – the electrical *current* that flows back and forth and sustains your company. You must be able to tap into that electrical current of cash flow when you need it most.

When you are flying on the trapeze, you must summon and channel your inner electrical currents to produce needed bursts of energy at the precise moments. Similarly, in your company, you must be able to tap into that electrical current of cash flow when you need it most.

The Truth About Cash Flow

Steel yourself for this: cash flow issues can happen to any company of any size at any time. I don't care if you're a $500,000 business or a $500 million business, at some point you will go through a cash flow crunch and need to have a backup plan at the ready. A lot of people think, "Oh, when I hit $50 million, I won't have a cash flow crunch anymore."

Expect the crunch: it's part of business. When it occurs, it doesn't mean you aren't good at business. It only means you need to better anticipate and prepare for the "crunchy" months far ahead of time.

CEOs often believe that once their businesses begin to generate seven-figure revenue, their cash flow problems will be over. That couldn't be further from reality. Consider the fact that every day you read in the news about a major business corporation laying off tens of thousands of employees. Giants such as Hewlett-Packard, General Motors, IBM, and AT&T have laid off 40,000 or more employees during the past few decades. Why? Largely because of cash-flow issues caused by a variety of circumstances.

Business owners must be well aware of the fact that being bigger doesn't make a company invulnerable. I readily admit to my clients that I have had my share of cash flow issues, even during some pretty large growth years. Why? You need to continually invest in your growth and sometimes it comes after a period of development in your revenue streams, systems, or your team. Or, it may be time for a course correction. Business and the market are changing so quickly these days that you must keep an eye on what is coming down the pike – not to be fearful, but to be smart. Some business owners seem relieved to hear that this is a relatively common occurrence and not necessarily a failing on their part.

Unfortunate, unpredictable things can and do happen when you least expect them. Costs and expenses rise as your company grows. Things break down and need replacement or repair. Your customers sometimes have cash flow issues of their own and can't (or won't) pay their bills on time. These are all normal lows of doing business and can deplete cash flow at any time.

As you get to know your business cycle, you will see which times of year are slower and which ones will yield large payments. This is why it is so important to track your cash flow and compare it year to year. Look for consistent cycles. For instance, some businesses are predictably seasonal and based on promotional holidays, such as Valentine's Day, Mother's Day, and Christmas. Or, a business such as a surfboard company is definitely going to be slower in the winter months. Cash flow planning and alternate methods of revenue generation need to be in place for that time period to help offset the dry spell.

In order to be prepared for your inevitable cash flow crunches, you must be as revenue-focused as possible through sales, marketing, and relationship-building efforts. If you can generate enough cash flow and reserves, you'll rely less upon money from investors and require fewer partners. You'll gain the immediate luxury of more freedom and independence and some wiggle room to experiment and fail before everything clicks.

On the other side of the equation for many companies are the systems. CEOs of various start-ups often feel that they can't function without a substantial amount of seed money to build their supportive systems. They end up rapidly depleting their cash because they don't understand how to build or scale a company. When the money diminishes, they have to start raising money all over again – which is a ton of work and an unbelievable amount of stress.

Before bringing in investors, I believe it's far better that you first build your systems, foundation, and revenue model on a shoestring to get your sales cranking. Once you have a flowing revenue stream – even if it's just a trickle at first – you can go after investors. This way you'll be more likely to spend the money where it needs to be spent, rather than on trying to figure out your business model and then blowing through everything provided to you. Steve Jobs did not have investors when he started out in that garage. He worked hard at selling a bunch of computers.

I'm convinced that many of the start-ups that fail do so because they receive gobs of money and react as if this is the end-all panacea – when it's not. What truly gets a start-up off the ground and flying are *sales, sales, and more sales*; the revenue model; the people; the product/service creation; cost-efficient, high ROI (return on investment) marketing; and the bare-bones systems that are just enough to bring in some revenue.

Know Your Numbers

I cannot tell you how many times I have worked with entrepreneurs who are not aware of their cost of *doing* business, percentage of growth (or loss) over time, and their net profit. Ultimately, the most important number is your profit: how much is left to walk home with at the end of the day.

As your company grows and scales, the bookkeeper and accountant that you started with may not be the ones that you continue with because those individuals are likely stuck in "scrimp-and-save" mode and not knowledgeable enough in bigger pictures areas of expanding into an enterprise, such as mergers and acquisitions (M&A). This is when it may be the time to bring on an experienced controller or chief cinancial officer (CFO), who has experience at the enterprise level and has been involved in big deal-making. Make sure you surround yourself with the right team to help you scale and add to your organization's body of knowledge.

Your Plates and Platters

Here's a simple technique to keeping your target numbers straight. Divide your financial goals into these three levels:

1. Your **Blue Plate Special Number** is the amount of revenue you must bring in to keep the lights on and meet the payroll.
2. Your **Silver Platter Number** is the amount of revenue that you need to breathe in your business. You can sleep at night comfortably without worrying about paying your bills. You have enough to invest in marketing and growth and to live a comfortable lifestyle, in which you can spend time doing what brings you joy with the people you love most.
3. Your **Gold Platter Number** usually comes into play as you scale, once your products, team, and systems are in place. This is where you see great traction in your growth, and your revenue and profits are on the rise. As they say in the Olympics, "Go for the gold, baby!"

Get clear on these three numbers, so you know what to reach for on a yearly, quarterly, and monthly basis – and then increase these numbers as you grow. Michelangelo said it perfectly: "The greater danger for most of us lies not in setting our aim too high and falling short; but in setting our aim too low, and achieving our mark."

It's All About the Sales

What do you suppose is the very first thing you should do every single day at work? Focus on sales, that's what!

The first three hours of every business day must be focused on sales (unless you have a sales team, and then it's a 24/7 deal) to generate cash flow that can help safeguard your business against any kind of inclement weather. This is time spent strategizing with your sales team, reaching out, seeking referrals, following up on leads, setting up meetings, and so on.

Rinse and repeat each and every day: *sales, sales, and more sales*! Remember, sales is sharing. If you truly believe you have the best product or service, get it into as many hands as possible.

> Your knowledge is less important than how much you truly care. That is why people do business with you. Make people feel good and they will buy into your ideas.
> —*Excerpt from my interview with Michael Bernoff, CEO of Human Communications, Inc. To watch the full interview, go to: www.ScaleorFail.com/bonus.*

Companies that are focused on revenue don't struggle with cash flow as much as others. As the CEO of your company, you always have to be the *chief convincing officer.* You must stay on top of your numbers and your sales team. Everyone in your company must be focused on the sales target, including the marketing department and your assistant. The entire organization must know the number of leads it takes to convert a sale, so you can work together as a team and make that target.

When my dad operated his women's clothing chain, every manager knew the daily sales goal. He was obsessed with the sales targets and constantly called every store to check in so that everyone stayed focused on the daily target. This was back in the day – but his company even had different color phones for each store for check-ins from the main warehouse: pink, green, turquoise, and so on. It might sound a bit overboard, but it worked.

Get a Credit Line

There's one lesson I learned early on that may sound a bit counterintuitive: Borrow money when you *don't* need it. It's a lot easier to get a loan when you're not in a desperate situation. Having the cash to draw from during a slow period – or during the float period between when you purchase your products and when you get paid – takes off a ton of pressure. Then you pay it back once you are busy again. Debt is not a bad thing when you're using it to grow. If you go on an unnecessary shopping spree buying things that have absolutely no return, that's one thing. Investing in your company – an asset with unlimited yield potential – is the smartest investment you can make.

Are You Ready to Scale?

When I am instructing a group on scaling, this is one of the first things I ask: "Is your business scalable?" The question hits most people sharply. It's surprising how rare business owners are asked (or ask themselves) this all-important question. If the CEO is doing all of the sales herself, for example, I can pretty much deduce right off the bat that the company is not super-scalable.

Being ready to scale means you have a system in place in which you have customers who are coming back to you on a regular basis and are generating reliable cash flow. Recurring revenue might include membership fees, subscriptions, courses, or payments for ongoing services.

There are so many ways to generate recurring revenue. For example, a lawn-mowing company might offer a special price for cutting grass on a weekly basis if a customer locks in for one year. Plus, the company could throw in a cross-sell for seasonal weeding, raking, or mulching. A membership program could be as low as $15 a month, but this adds up if you have hundreds or even thousands of people paying that amount. It may not necessarily be the core of your business – it's an extra – but it provides something additional and sustaining.

Once you have a sustainable, recurring model and know where the cash flow is going to come from, your business starts to snowball. It starts small, but gets bigger and bigger and gains momentum as it moves forward.

You've probably heard of *valuation*. In simple terms, this is the value of your business should you decide to sell it. If your business generates *static revenue* – meaning earnings from a one-time sale – that would be considered a *one-time valuation*. However, if your business model involves *recurring revenue*, such as monthly or annually, then it's a *three-to-five valuation*. This means that it's worth three times the value when you go to sell it than if you just had static revenue because the sales happen on an ongoing, predictable basis. Venture capitalists salivate over the growth and ROI possibilities of businesses that have recurring revenue.

So ask yourself: *Is your business ready to scale? Is your snowball gaining speed? Is it doing so on its own with minimum additional effort?*

The Yellow Brick Roads to Scaling

There are several ways to safeguard cash flow while scaling your business. You need to be creative and nimble in order to recognize and take advantage of these strategies. Depending on your type of business, you might be able to merge your current strategies with new ones. Take a look at the Scalable Strategies worksheet (Figure 3.1) to see if any of these might apply to your business. Brainstorm with your team to see if there are any others they can come up with.

Leverage It

Once you have your model nailed down, you can leverage it into different markets. That could potentially mean expanding into different physical locations, marketing your product or services to a different customer base, or adding a natural extension onto something your business is already doing.

This is how the grocery business works: basically, the large food and beverage companies buy space. It's all about buying real estate.

PINNACLE GLOBAL NETWORK®
THE WORLD LEADER IN SCALING BUSINESSES

Scalable Strategies

- replicate your talent with a **team**
- get your customers to **buy more** often
- add **services** to a product
- **membership** sites
- **certification** programs
- monthly **subscription** service
- **licensing** your signature products, programs or services
- **retainers**
- online **courses**
- **service** plans
- your own **technology**
- national **distribution** team
- **expand** globally
- same model, new **locations**
- **buy** your competitors
- **manufacture** in house
- turn a cost center into a **profit** center
  (ex. turn your social media into a service for others)

Brainstorm Your Scale Strategies...

© Allison Maslan International

Figure 3.1: Determine what strategies you can add to grow your cash flow.

In my company, we realized that we weren't going to get any more space for our beverage than maybe 10% to 15%. We needed to come up with cash in order to grow. But we were never going to be able to write $30–60 million checks for that.

I decided that my growth was going to be capped if we decided to play in this game. We started doing business with Amazon and did really well in that channel. One day at a meeting with them, I said, "I really want to understand who's buying."

They said, "Well, we can't give you the names, but we'll give you a glimpse of who's buying."

It turned out that the people who were buying our product were also buying diabetes monitors. They were buying pregnancy-related items. "Great," I said. "I want to go out and talk to them."

The Amazon team said, "No, we're not able to give you that data."

It was at that moment that I realized that I didn't have control of my customer. I didn't know anything about my customer at Publix, Whole Foods, or anyplace else, either.

I had grown up in a place where data was so important to me, and yet suddenly I didn't know who my customer was. I went back to my board, and I said, "We're going to launch our website at drinkhint.com, and we're going to start selling cases of Hint, and if consumers want us to sell it to them on auto shipment every week, or every month, then we're going to do that. If they want to change flavors, we're going to do that, too."

I didn't know if it was going to work, but I thought, Let's just throw it out there and see what happens.

Two and a half years later, this channel became almost 40% of our overall business. The great thing is that when we decided to launch a product like sunscreen, we were able to go back to our database.

We have a lot of consumers who are coming to us and saying, "If you guys do those kind of trials, we would love to be a part of it."

When I talk to other food and beverage companies about their online businesses I ask: "Oh, are you guys online?"

They say, "Oh, yeah, we sell through Amazon."

This is fine, but they don't know who their customers are or anything about them. They don't actually understand what kind of problems they can solve for their customers. To them, it's really just about the dollar sales. This is important, but it's not everything.

—Excerpt from my interview with Kara Goldin, CEO and founder of Hint Inc. For the full interview, go to: www.ScaleorFail.com/bonus.

Here's a quick example. A client of mine, Lisa Miller, who ran a photography business for several years called me one day and told me that her husband was recovering from a recent stroke. Then she said, "This was his wake-up call. He is serious about going after his dream of running a winery." I said, "Fantastic. Let's make it happen!" Together they created Koi Zen Winery, where they crush their own grapes and bottle their own signature brand of select wines. Now, four short years later, they have more than doubled their space and won several international wine awards, including double gold and best of class for his 2015 Malbec. One of the smartest moves they made was starting a subscription-based wine club that now has over 500 members. (I am one of them, of course!) Limiting their growth to one retail location would not be scalable; however, with their own brand of wine and monthly recurring revenue of their wine club, the skies are the limit!

Happy Baby, Happy Parents

One of my clients created Happi Tummi, a product designed to help infants with stomach ailments sleep better. The device consists of a waistband and herbal pouch containing lavender, chamomile, lemon grass, peppermint, spearmint, wheat, and flax seed. When heated, the herbs release healing properties that provide almost immediate relief of colic, gas, and other chronic digestive issues.

My client was able to make a slight shift and create a whole new market of business by taking the same idea – the same product with a few modifications – and also target adults who are experiencing stomach discomfort. If it worked for babies, why wouldn't it also work for adults? They have stomach ailments, too! She's leveraged her successful product for another customer and opened the door to a lot more cash flow. This is how you scale.

Replicate Yourself

If only we could clone ourselves – wouldn't that be wonderful? We would get so many more things done! Well, until science figures out how to accomplish this, we must improvise.

Business owners often cling to the misguided belief that they are the only ones who can handle certain tasks. They are also convinced that they are the only ones who can manage certain clients, who want to work only with them. If you are one of these owners, this is your ego speaking. Yes, there are things that you can do (talent) and know (experience) that your team may not have – at first. It's up to you to open up your mind to the idea that you shouldn't be handling so many tasks and client relationships yourself. If you hired the right people, you must trust that they can be trained and entrusted with your wisdom to do the same things you do.

It all needs to be systematized, so that your team understands how you operate, how you work with clients and customers, and how you want your products represented to the outside world. Once you have been "replicated" and your team is doing the things that you used to do, you have the time and bandwidth to scale your business in a number of different ways – including replicating yourself and your team as you establish various business extensions.

I worked with a company for a few years that owns a healthy food delivery service in Fort Worth, Texas. That is a low margin business because the ingredients are expensive and there is only so much people will pay for food. She was working so hard – even building a team – but profits were only inching along. I helped her brainstorm and develop a program to train other personal chefs across the country how to build a successful business. Not only did she win Personal Chef of the Year, but that business ended up bringing in at least three times more revenue than her food delivery business.

This is a great example of how to replicate, multiply, and give back, all at the same time. It's interesting because I often find that the most creative revenue ideas come when you hit a wall – hard. Stress can be a good thing when it forces you to get creative and think in a new way to come up with quick solutions. If you're moving along okay, even at a slower pace, what will compel you internally to think outside of the box? Nothing.

Hiring Forward

People have occasionally come up to me and asked these questions:

- How do you know when you're ready to hire?
- How much money must you have in the bank before you hire?

The answer that I generally provide is that most businesses don't have a chunk of change sitting in their bank accounts to cover their new employees' salaries for a long period of time. When you hire the right employees, they will pay for themselves in increased revenue or productivity. If this position will help you produce a lucrative product faster or drive greater sales and revenue, your company has an opportunity to grow to a much larger scale. If you hold back on hiring to fill these positions – which might be sales oriented or on the creative side – you may end up missing great revenue opportunities.

Even adding an administrative position will create more productivity, taking work off your plate to assist getting your products or service out to the marketplace faster, with better customer service behind it. What happens next? Reorders, referrals, and happier clients for longer periods of time. Your lifetime value of a client goes up, and so do your profits.

Look for the holes in your company, and also in which areas you want to grow. Adding the right support there is like adding Miracle Grow to your business. It's not as if I have six months of salary sitting in the bank for staffing. But I've found that, when I take a risk and add a key position in and hire the right person, the money always comes. The business grows. I call this *hiring forward*.

> For me, as a top line operator, I hire ahead of time. I know more is always coming.
> —*Excerpt from my interview with Gary Vaynerchuk, CEO, VaynerMedia. For the full interview, go to: www.ScaleorFail.com/bonus.*

When you hire forward, you identify an area of business growth, onboard someone into a brand new role to own it, and then watch your business organically grow. Your mind may try to tell you that you are adding expense in an uncharted area which makes it "high risk," but that's not the case. It's not about recruiting someone who will add to your overhead. You do this so your business will get to the next level. If you're waiting for that money to magically appear in your account on its own, it's never going to happen. You need to bring in people with talent and contacts so you can extend your business vision. Then your cash flow will soar.

Get Your Customers to Buy from You More Often

This may seem obvious, but you need to get your customers to buy from you more often. Sometimes the upselling opportunities are staring you in the face and you don't think to take advantage of them. Offering existing customers a service plan or a warranty is one obvious way of upselling. Car manufacturers do this all the time with maintenance agreements.

Statistically speaking, on average existing clients account for 41% of your income. They are apt to spend *five times more than new clients* because you already have a relationship with them. They already trust you and know what you can do. Many customers love the idea of a "one-stop shop" where they can have all of their needs provided by one partner or vendor. Wherever possible, you should strive to become that one-stop shop.

New customers can be cagey and skeptical and often want to take things slowly, one step at a time. You have to prove yourself and your company's value. Often it takes time to figure out the onboarding process with a new customer. From your standpoint, you have no idea if this new client will be a good one or not and pay bills on time.

With your existing customers, look both inside and outside the box to answer these questions:

- What three additional products or services can you find to upsell or cross-sell?
- What are they getting somewhere else that you can offer at better quality, with a higher level of service, or at a better price?
- What products or services do you currently provide free of charge that could be bundled for a fee?

With regard to the last point, above, are you giving away too much for free because you are afraid of losing a customer? Trust me when I say this: *Free is not a sustainable business model.*

You should be working to monetize every aspect of your business. You are in business to make a great profit. This is how you will scale, give back to your team and their families, and take that leap from entrepreneur to enterprise.

One of my clients, an event planner, also books hotel rooms for out-of-town attendees of major events. While speaking to her I realized that she and her team were spending hours upon hours on this service and not charging for it, losing valuable time (which is money) and significant potential revenue. It is great to give over value, but leaving an entire revenue stream is crazy-making. I told her to package this service with her main on the table event-planning service and offer it as her premium product for a higher-priced revenue offering.

When it comes to shaking the trees for revenue from your existing customers, there are many things you can do. If you are in doubt about where to start, look at other industries, such as credit-card companies, hotels, and airlines, which constantly offer special memberships, VIP perks, and loyalty programs. It seems as if every day Starbucks has a different incentive to lure you into the store and buy coffee: iced drinks $2 after 2:00, or extra bonus stars if you order the macchiato on a certain day, and so on.

What can you offer to entice your existing customers to buy more?

The Product Pyramid

The Product Pyramid is a multitiered approached to bringing in customers at every level. Presently, you may be hitting on only one or two of these levels – but you have the potential to build your customer base to establish relationships with customers in every single one of them.

Let's stick with the coffee example, since we were just reflecting on Starbucks. Suppose you're a coffee customer who wants to make a good, no-frills cup of coffee at home. There are many ways to go about doing this. If you just want something down-and-and-dirty right away, you'd go online and buy a coffee maker for maybe $79. Done.

But let's say you're a real coffee aficionado. You love the experience of coffee and want the absolute best shot of espresso every morning right in your home. You don't mind taking the time to go to Starbucks or another coffee vendor to check out all the brewing options. You end up spending $2,999 on a top-of-the-line coffee maker that features the most innovative technology so that you can make you the perfect cup of espresso.

All of these two extreme ends of the customer spectrum – as well as the ones in the middle – apply to your business. There should be a customer for every level of your offerings.

Now take a look at the Product Pyramid worksheet (Figure 3.2). You can upload this at: www.ScaleorFail.com/bonus.

At the top level of the pyramid is your free offering. This is how you get people into your database. This is where customers enter your world and learn about what you can do. They learn about your value, quality, and wisdom, as well as develop trust in your business.

At the next level, take your main revenue steam and consider what you could add to it to give it more touch points with your customers. If you would like to double or triple your price, for example, what bells and whistles could you add on that would match, or even exceed, that extra value? Everyone loves a premium service, and I guarantee there are plenty of customers out there for you within this tier.

In the third tier, you are thinking about what you could create that has a few touch points. Think of it as a watered-down version of what your business offers. Often you are bundling and packaging an assortment of items that's more in total but less than how you would price them individually. The customer sees this as a bargain and a way to scoop up a range of offerings all at once.

PINNACLE GLOBAL NETWORK®
THE WORLD LEADER IN SCALING BUSINESSES

THE PRODUCT PYRAMID

free opt-in
- FREE CD,
AUDIO, VIDEO SERIES
- WHITEPAPER
- E-BOOK
- ASSESSMENT • PODCAST...

low level buy-in
- BOOK • WORKBOOK • E-BOOK
- LOW-END RETAIL PRODUCT
- MONTHLY CD'S • MEMBERSHIP CLUB
- EVENT • TOOLS...

mid-range buy-in
- COACHING OR CONSULTING PACKAGES
- WORKSHOP • DVD / AUDIO PROGRAM
- TELECLASS / VIDEO / WEBINAR SERIES
- ONLINE/OFFLINE COURSES • MID-RANGE RETAIL PRODUCT

high level buy-in
- HIGH-END COACHING OR CONSULTING PACKAGE
- HIGH-END RETAIL PRODUCT • LICENSING FRANCHISE
- HIGH-END EVENTS • CERTIFICATION PROGRAMS
- HIGH-END GROUP PROGRAM OR VIP SERVICE

success!

free opt-in

low level buy-in

mid-range buy-in

high level buy-in

success!

© Allison Maslan International

Figure 3.2: Engaging customers at every level of interest.

At the bottom of the pyramid is the "concierge" level, where you have earned "high-level buy-in" from customers. You have built a relationship and earned their trust: Now is your time to shine and show them what you can really do! This is where you create a true experience for your customers and add extra attention and luxurious choices. One example might be to create a high-end event just for these elite customers. This is your chance to exceed expectations and wow them.

There may be some customers who stop at the second or third tier. That's okay! The main thing is that your business model includes opportunities to welcome customers now or later at every level. They could buy the $79 coffee maker, the $2,999 coffee maker, or a variety of coffee makers in between. In the middle of these offerings, you may bundle in specialty espresso beans, coffee grinders, fancy espresso cups and saucers, or whatever makes sense for your particular business and customer.

Licensing

Another great way to expand a business without stretching yourself too thin is through licensing. Some business owners feel that licensing their brands, products, or services is the equivalent of giving away their children – but it's not. If anything, it's a less taxing way to *make more children* (i.e., products, services, etc.) without having to do any of the work. Once an agreement is done, licensing becomes primarily a bookkeeping function that brings in regular income.

A few years ago, I created an idea for software while I was relaxing near the water with my husband in Laguna Beach. From this burst of creativity, I went on to develop Interactive Life Coach to help business owners stay on track with their goals and dreams. Several people liked it so much they wanted to license and white-label it. I had no problem with the arrangement. For me, it was revenue for doing hardly anything. For the licensees, it was a way to have a proven product ready without having to start from square one. Software is a tremendous platform for scaling, since your investment is primarily in the initial build and overhead does not need to grow at the rate of your expansion.

In my organization's Pinnacle Global Network, we work with Jon and Gila Kurtz, the cofounders of Dog Is Good, a lifestyle brand for people who love dogs. When the couple began working with us, they were primarily creating revenue through wholesaling their products to retail stores. At the time, Gila had lost her passion for the business because she was stuck in a cycle of working on areas of the business that did not make her sing. In mentoring her and her husband to build a much more scalable enterprise, my team found several ways to help them develop other revenue streams without adding tremendous overhead, so they could scale. First, we helped guide them to expand their licensing program to other product manufacturers, which has created dramatic financial growth and has exponentially expanded their brand recognition. Gila was able to step back a few steps from working in the business and create Fur-Covered Wisdom, where she shares her passion about the power of dogs and personal growth. This rebooted her passion for building her company. We also helped them design their own Signature Exhibitor Program, which became known as the Dog Is Good Mobile Pop-Up Shop and has resulted in an entire sales force of individuals hosting pop-up shops of Dog Is Good products across the country.

> I can't even begin to tell you what is happening with this program! It's giving me an entirely new meaning in this business. I feel I'm really making a difference for these individuals who are coming on board.
>
> —*Gila Kurtz, cofounder, Dog Is Good*

On top of all this, after applying my Pinnacle Signature Program Method, Gila and Jon developed Dig Delivery Auto-Ship – a monthly subscription program for retailers. This puts their purchases on autopilot! No more one-time sales. They now have recurring revenue, which is a business owner's dream and perfect a formula for scaling. Through all of this expansion and awareness, their online sales more than doubled.

Retainers

Retainers are an excellent way for you to generate recurring revenue and reliable cash flow. This is where you can be creative in terms of thinking about what services you might provide that your clients consider valuable on a regular (i.e., monthly) basis. Rather than getting paid per project or by the hour, you are receiving a standard payment every month ($2,500, $5,000, etc.). It could be in the form of a marketing retainer, a public relations retainer, a consulting retainer, and so on. People with small tech companies can offer a range of extra services on retainer – from managing servers, databases, and websites to repairing and/or ordering software and hardware.

Best of all, when you are on retainer you don't have to feel like you are nitpicking and justifying every hour of work you put in. Then you have the freedom to be more creative and provide a higher-level of value and ongoing support, resulting in happier clients – which is what we all want.

Some people get caught up in the "dollars for hours" model, which is very difficult to scale. One of the things I teach clients is how they can create their own signature programs and add more value to their offerings. This means you can bill *more per month* than what you would earn on an hourly or project-by-project basis. Instead of your clients thinking of you in terms of an hourly freelancer, they see you as an authority – an expert. In reality, they are not paying you for your time. You are worth much more than that. What they are really paying you for is your wisdom, years of experience and study, capabilities, skills, ideas, insight, and the proprietary process that you have developed.

These combined processes and unique style are what set you apart from everyone else. When you pull of your processes together in a sequential format and name each process in a unique way, the value of your offering goes way up. For instance, the SCALEit Method is a compilation of my years of in-the-trenches experience, solutions to challenges, and step-by-step processes to add clarity, ease, and faster breakthroughs and results in a more streamlined process of scaling your company. That is very different than throwing a hodge-podge of knowledge or services at your client.

Franchising

Once you have your model down and have established a couple of locations that build your profitability, you can sell your concept, systems, and marketing to others to create franchises. All you need to do in this case is develop a "business-in-a-box" that franchisees can step into and run and then help them find prime locations.

The pros of this are pretty obvious: You save the time and investment in starting up each individual new business location. Once a franchise gets going, you get to count the residuals.

It is super-important that you have a strong support system in place for your franchisees. They often do not have business experience, and that is why they are buying a franchise in the first place. The more support you offer in the way of negotiating leases, marketing, and sales, the more successful they will be; this will result in more people wanting to buy more franchises. Too many franchisors do not offer enough support to their franchisees. Sadly, this sets franchisees up to fail.

Also, franchises can be unpredictable in terms of knowing which ones will catch on, spread into other areas, and have long-term staying power. The biggest franchises – McDonald's, 7-Eleven, Dunkin' Donuts, and the UPS Store – have all become monster successes and have withstood fierce competition over the years, as well as thriving during changing economic climates.

On the flip side, it's all too easy for a franchise to plummet while expanding, as was the case with Subway. The sandwich chain went through the roof during the Great Recession, adding 2,300 locations from 2007 to 2009 and another 4,000 in the United States over the next five years. But then things started to slip and locations began to close. Why? They expanded too aggressively and lowered their prices too much. The model might have worked during the Recession, but it didn't sustain itself after that.

If your business is a "monkey business" in which you are not reliant on skilled workers, the franchise model will have more success. The way to build it is with area developers in mind, not as a onesie and twosie strategy.

Area developers are experienced business people who purchase large territories and develop them on a timely schedule. This helps create the brand footprint quicker. It's easy to get carried away once you have a taste of success. Test locations out in the right territories to ensure the model fits everywhere and can weather – or even take advantage of – any economic storm.

Certification Programs

Perhaps your business lends itself to creating a certification program. If you and your team have expertise in an area, you can build a program that trains others to become experts as well. This is a terrific way to scale because you are getting people to sign up for a number of sessions or events so they may fulfill the certification obligation, which means consistent cash flow with people paying up front. This also expands the reach of your craft, positively impacting so many more people than you or your team can do on your own.

Get creative and develop a certification program in an untapped area. For example, I have a client who owns a cold-storage company. She's created a certification program to help contractors become certified in cold storage. Nobody has ever done this before, and now she has an entirely new revenue stream for her company. Not only that, she has confidence in knowing she has a team of well-trained contractors to provide their cold-storage methods.

When I built the Homeopathic Academy of Southern California in 1999, I created a three-year certification program that trained hundreds of homeopaths to go out and improve thousands of people's lives. I knew that I could see only so many clients on my own and, if I was going to make a significant difference, I needed to expand my reach. I sold the school in 2005. Because the curriculum and systems were in place, it continued to support and build the homeopathic community for years to come. When a labor of love does good things for people exponentially and creates great profit, you have a winning model.

You are probably thinking: "Aren't I creating competition for myself by doing this?" Maybe. Then again, some of the people who become trained and certified might be so good you want to hire them yourself. If this isn't the case, certifying others to become competition is still a lot more lucrative than soliciting new clients one by one. And, if you're the company creating the certification process, you are now elevated as the authority in your industry, resulting in higher fees and much more business. As you certify, you shift from one to many, making it a perfect model to scale.

Buy Your Competitors

Sometimes the best way to scale is to buy your competition. They have a team that knows your industry and a built-in customer base. Occasionally, with the art of negotiation working for you, you can catch a company at just the right time.

This can create a quick boost to your growth without years of building. Whether this competitor has been a thorn in your side or a supportive peer, this smart purchase will give you a big leg up in the scaling process.

One of my clients owns a machine-calibrating company. One way they've scaled is by buying several competitors who do the same exact thing. They've rid themselves of their competition and grown their businesses, to boot. This is a quick way to scale without starting at ground zero.

There are challenges in buying other companies. First, of course, there are the financials and making 100% certain that the prospects are profitable and solid and the books are clean. Then you have to make sure the new team fits in with your culture and that the employees are motivated and skillful with your processes. Once you employ them, you must train them and make them feel as if they are an equal part of the team so they can get on board with your Big Picture Vision.

Your Business Blueprint: Marketing and Cash Flow

Business without marketing is no business at all. You won't have cash flow if you aren't getting the word out about your product or service. If you know how to reach and market to your customer, you can pretty much build any type of business successfully. I am so grateful that my first company was an advertising/PR firm. I had no idea what I was doing in the early years. It was education by fire (and there were lots of fires). I have been able to apply that marketing knowledge to all of my nine subsequent companies.

The first order of business is targeting the *right* customer. You need to identify:

- Who is your ideal customer?
- What does she/he desire?
- Can you reach her/him?
- Is this customer willing to pay for your product or service?

- Who is the competition?
- What is their message and how can you do it better?

If you can't answer the above questions, you'll go too broad or too narrow with your marketing and will completely miss the target. So many marketers bang their heads against a wall because they are trying to get the wrong customer to buy. It's way too easy to keep throwing money away like that.

My Perfect Client Decoder

Take a look at the worksheet entitled My Perfect Client Decoder (Figure 3.3), copy it, and fill in the blanks on a separate sheet of paper. Essentially, you are looking to identify your customer demographic and psychographic. It's not just honing in on obvious things such as gender and age, it's also pinpointing your customers' phase in life. Where are they currently? What are their buying habits and their values? Why do they buy?

You might, for example, identify that your customer is in the life phase of having babies. Well, that is a pretty big age range; moms can be anywhere between their 20s and 50s. As you can imagine, marketing to a 20-something is quite different from marketing to a 50-something, even though they share the commonality of having babies.

Once you have a crystal clear picture of your customer, then you can figure out how and where to reach them and the best way to catch their attention and communicate with them. One of the easiest, least expensive, and most accurate ways of doing this is to go direct to the source. Take your best clients to lunch. Tell them they are your favorite clients and why you love working with them. Ask if they would be open to your interviewing them to learn more about the the their patterns because you want more clients just like them!

PINNACLE
G L O B A L
N E T W O R K®
THE WORLD LEADER
IN SCALING BUSINESSES

My PERFECT
CLIENT Decoder

Gender _____

Married/Single _____

Age Range _____

Income Level

_____

Education Level

_____

Where Do They
Live? _____

_____

Where Do They
Vacation?

_____

_____

What Are Their
Health Habits?

_____

_____

_____

What Phase Of Life
Are They In ?

_____

What Do They Do For Fun? _____

_____

What Associations Or Organizations Do
They Belong To? _____

_____

What Non-Profits Do They Support?

_____

Which Social Media Do They Use?

_____

What Publications Or Blogs Do They
Read? _____

_____

Describe Their Personality _____

_____

_____

What Problems Keep Them Up At Night?

_____

What Do They Want The Most?

_____

How Do They Feel About Your Business/
Industry/Product/Service?

_____

How Can You Solve Their Problems?

_____

© Allison Maslan International

Figure 3.3: Identifying the perfect client.

Find out the following:

- What blogs do they read?
- What books do they read?

- What sporting events do they attend?
- What hobbies are they interested in?
- What charities are they involved in?
- What TV shows do they watch?
- What things excite them?
- What things make them angry? (This is where their passion and pain lies. If you can speak to this, your chances of capturing their attention go way up.)

Once you have figured these things out, then you must decide on the vehicle, or the marketing medium, that you're going to use to reach them – whether it's social media, pay-per-click ads, TV commercials, email lists, or some other method.

Your Database Is Your Gold

One of the best, most effective kinds of marketing is one that can be automated so you're developing relationships with your customers and building on them over time. Pay close attention to this: Automating the relationship does not mean setting things on autopilot. It *does* mean knowing your customers so well that you have identified their interests, can market to them on a dime, and always have them on your hook to buy more.

Continuity marketing programs accomplish this exceptionally well. Similar to the offer process, from entry level to premium choices, mentioned earlier in this chapter, by giving customers an opportunity to opt-in their contact information for a free gift that is of great value, you begin to build your database, which is your gold. You don't own your list on social media. The social media platforms do. When they opt-in to *your* list, this actually increases the valuation of your company when you go to sell it. When Borders Group national book chain went out of business, Barnes & Noble did not want their furniture; instead, they bought their database! Once you have established this connection, you can build a long-term relationship that ultimately turns into a customer. After a period of nurturing with great educational, entertaining, and authentic content that speaks to the customers' pain points, you can ask for the sale, starting with a lower-level offering and building on up to your premium offer. By continually staying in front of them, by being a giver of good content, great service, and following through on your promises, your customers will continue to come back for more at a higher price.

Perhaps you are old enough to remember one of most famous of these, Columbia House, which back in the 1970s and 1980s offered records and cassettes for only a penny apiece. For your investment of only one penny, you could get something like thirteen records. After that, you were obligated to purchase records at full price – by which point you'd pretty much exhausted any music they had that you'd actually want to hear.

The genius of Columbia House wasn't just that they were reeling you in to buy all those records. What they were really doing was building their customer database (okay, at the time it was known as a "mailing list") in order to create relationships and sell more stuff to the same customers. In all likelihood, they were probably selling those mailing lists as well.

Earlier in this chapter I stressed that "free isn't a business model." This only applies to your products and services, not to your marketing. Think about what you can offer of value to your customers free of charge that costs you pennies, but has great upside when those customers come back to you later for more. Don't be afraid to share your great wisdom, ideas, insights, in the form of downloads, so that they can get to know the value of your expertise. This positions you as the expert in your arena and sets you apart from your competition. They'll say, "Wow, Allison really offers some interesting things. I'm not ready to buy, but when I am she's the one."

Nurturing trust at this stage is crucial. If you are too aggressive and push too hard for the sale, you risk sounding desperate and putting people off. It's okay if they don't buy from you right when they receive your free gift. The fact that you aren't being too pushy is actually appreciated by most customers and then they want to buy from you.

Think about it this way: Would you ask someone to get married on the first date? (I retract this – maybe it can happen. One of the business mentors on my team met a woman at a bar in Las Vegas. They got married that night and they've been happily married for eight years. There are outliers to everything, I suppose.)

Raving Fans Become Your Sales Force

I'm not going to get into the nuances of which social media platform is the best to use for marketing purposes because they are changing all the time, along with our technology. Whichever platform you choose to use, depending on your target market, you need to focus on how to generate buzz and excitement and build a *raving fan community*.

The important note here is "the unexpected gift of support." Most people get a sense of when to expect promotions or giveaways, but when you give your prospect or customer a forward-thinking product or service that is in line with what he or she desires, needs, and expectations and then give him just a little bit more, you're well on your way toward creating a raving fan.

When you have dedicated, faithful customers online or offline, these individuals automatically become voices for your product. In a sense, these raving fans become part of your sales force. They offer five-star reviews, comment and share your online content, and go out of their way to support you and introduce you to their favorite connections. This is how you build a tribe and a movement gets started.

When I began putting a good portion of my marketing dollars into more customer love and appreciation, the referrals and renewals jumped up dramatically. This is one of the best returns on investment you can get – and it feels rewarding, too.

How Much Do I Invest in Marketing?

When determining how much to invest in your marketing, you first must back up and determine your Customer Lifetime Value (CLTV), which is a prediction of the net profit attributed to the entire future relationship with your customer. Here is a simple formula:

average value of a sale × number of repeat transactions × average retention time in months or years for a typical customer = CLTV

For instance, if your customer lifetime value is $3,000, and it costs you $500 to acquire that customer, you will happily spend that $500. The point is, you'll never know how to develop a solid marketing budget unless you know what the return on your investment needs to be. This knowledge is vital because it will help you make marketing decisions based on the reality of your own numbers, rather than the promises of some new media program.

The Richness Is in the Relationship

I invest a lot of time and money in building relationships. In over 30 years of business, relationship building is at the top of the list with regard to how I grow my companies; it's also one of my favorite parts of being a CEO. I invest well over $150,000 a year on getting in front of the right people. This includes being in a high-level mastermind – which I will soon explain – and attending events or cruises filled with influencers, the people who can open doors for you. One right connection can save you years of trying to reinvent the wheel.

Greek shipping magnate Aristotle Onassis was known for telling the story of what he would do if he lost his fortune. He said he would take on three jobs. From his earnings, he would carve out and save $500. He would spend all of it on one expensive meal – just to get close to someone who could open doors for him. Sitting next to the right person and making a connection with him or her is the fastest way to create your fortune.

What tribes are, is a very simple concept that goes back 50 million years. It's about leading and connecting people and ideas. And it's something that people have wanted forever.
—*Seth Godin, bestselling author, marketing authority, and entrepreneur*

I'm constantly giving my clients strategies intended to help them get in front of the right people. "One connection can potentially be worth millions of dollars."

Make a list of some big goals you would like to accomplish. Think about someone whom you may know or do not know that could possibly help you make these goals a reality through his or her own resources or network. This may be a well-connected business owner, a celebrity, or anyone who is well known in your industry. First, make the intention that you will meet that person. Then research the best ways to make that connection. This could be through an introduction, a charity, an event, an email, or even a letter or phone call. It may take a combination of phone calls and emails. Get creative! It may not happen overnight, but persistence always pays off.

When I had my ad agency, I wanted to meet Larry Lawrence, the owner of Charlotte Russe clothing chain. I called his office at least a dozen times without success. Then, one day he finally called me back and said, "I am calling you, so you will stop calling me." He ended up becoming my biggest client and we helped Charlotte Russe take their stores from 15 to 50. I made enough money to put a down payment on a home within six months.

Being a connector also means taking the initiative to connect other people without any specific benefit to you – except that you develop a reputation as someone who helps others and then it becomes even more likely that people will help you without you even trying. If you want people to connect to you, you must reciprocate and be a connector for them as well. For example, if you know someone who just finished writing a book and you happen to be good friends with a literary agent, you might introduce the two.

Life gives to the giver and takes from the taker.
—*Joe Polish, marketing authority, entrepreneur, and innovator*

Joint Ventures: Powerhouse Connectors

Joint ventures are an excellent marketing strategy that can generate revenue and lead to brand awareness through the connections themselves. We've seen these work on a grand scale when two juggernauts connect, such Oprah and Starbucks. Talk about a Goliath of connections! It was so brilliant in its simplicity: Oprah brought her Chai Tea to Starbucks and then advertised the product.

In the above example, Oprah creates the product and donates her time and energy as spokesperson; however, she doesn't need to worry about distribution or sales. On the flipside, Starbucks provides the distribution and sales outlets without having to create a new product that may or may not catch on with customers; in turn, Oprah's brand and popularity brings customers into their stores. A clear-cut win-win.

In your business, think about parties outside your industry that might benefit from a connection with your brand. In turn, be certain that what you have to offer is equally as desirable and beneficial to the other party.

Networking does not mean meeting people; it means becoming the type of person other people want to meet.
—Jay Conrad Levinson and Jeannie Levinson,
authors of Guerrilla Marketing

Factoring

If your profit margin allows for it, you can factor your accounts receivable at 4–5% of your committed invoices. The way this works is that you receive money up front from the factoring company and then they collect the payment from your client. For instance, if your Net 30 invoice is $1,000, the factoring company will pay you $960 and collect $1000 from the client. You receive payment faster, so you can use that money to buy inventory or even reinvest it for more business. It is an easier qualifying strategy because they are looking at the strength of your customer, rather than your financial statements.

Presales Is Where It's At

Amazon does it. Apple does it. Nearly every innovative company does it: preselling their products before they are ready and available. Giving customers a tease or taste of coming generates curiosity and buzz. Apple is brilliant at tantalizing its customers into jumping to buy the next generation iPhone. In addition, preselling gets your production and sales teams pumped in anticipation, which leads to great things happening up until the very end. You also gain the benefit of getting insights into customer reactions early, which can help you forecast inventory to meet demand.

Many of the products we have sold in my companies started as presales. Do your marketing first, then deliver your product. You can perfect it along the way. There is a saying that I love:

"Build the plane while you fly it." In other words: Don't wait until it's all finished and tied with a bow to start selling the product. Get your marketing going, create a buzz of excitement, and attract some cash flow. Then, when your launch happens, you'll already be sitting pretty with sales.

Are You Undervaluing Your Products?

While I'm an advocate of promotional discounts in some instances and other marketing incentives, I am equally as dedicated to opposing pricing models that are too low and undervalue your products and services. Some business owners become afraid that customers won't buy from them unless they are priced lower than their competitors. The truth is, you may get a customer through a lower price offering – but you won't *keep* a customer this way. You want to attract customers who truly value you and what you offer. If you drop your prices too low, what you are projecting to the marketplace is that you don't believe your product is worth that much. Studies have shown that customers believe higher-priced products are more attractive and more valuable. Timex is said to be a better-made watch than Rolex. However, Rolex has built a brand identity that expresses longevity and success, which allows them to charge a lot more. People will invest to be associated with a brand of such stature and prestige.

A few years back, I was speaking on the phone with a woman who offered a workshop I was interested in attending. She quoted a price of several thousands of dollars. Although it was expensive, I was still highly interested because I believed the workshop offered something that would help me immensely. I paused for a moment to think about it. That silence must have made her nervous because she dropped her price – and then again a few seconds later. In that moment, I completely lost interest. She did not have confidence in her product; therefore, I lost confidence in her ability to deliver it. If she had held her price, I have no doubt I would have made the purchase.

The key is that the price must match the value you're offering. Would $1 extra per unit matter to the customer? $10? $100? $1,000? If your customers want to work with you and care about you, they will stay with you and trust your judgment on pricing. If one of my dedicated vendors were to raise her prices, I won't just jump ship and go somewhere else. In most cases, I trust my vendors so much I would believe that the increase is justified and that they deserve it.

Your goal is to expand your margin as much as possible. Match your fee with the value you are offering. If you're working day and night and not making money, you're not charging enough.

Being Change Adaptive to Make Some Change

Lastly, when it comes to marketing or any plan of action, you need to be flexible and change on a dime when your market changes or your strategy is not working. Business is a living, breathing, ever-changing dynamic, so you must always be testing and tracking your metrics to see what is working and what is not. Just because a marketing strategy worked for years does not mean it will continue to do so. Businesses get left in the dust or disrupted all the time because they do not stay nimble. Look at what is working and what is not. Then be willing to move quickly.

Mike, my husband (yes, I did finally find my forever Prince Charming), has run a company called CA Office Liquidators in the office furniture industry for over three decades. When large companies are moving or going out of business, his company buys their used furniture (cubicles and workstations) and then sells them to other companies. A few years ago, he realized his competitive advantage was his unique method of brokering the entire inventories to other new and used office dealers versus retailing the furniture in smaller sales to the end users. This was much more profitable and enjoyable rather than dealing with the onesie, twosie sales to the end user. This sharp pivot drastically reduced his overhead because he did not need massive warehouse space. The end result was that it increased his profits by 40% within six months.

In your business, you must be willing to monitor the results of your cash flow and marketing tactics and react appropriately in the moment. Often a small shift can be life changing for all involved.

Chapter Summary: You've Got This!

- DON'T wait to prepare your business for inevitable cash flow crunches.
- DO focus on sales the first three hours of each day.
- DO try to expand your business by creating a recurring business model.
- DO try one or more of these methods to drive cash flow: Leveraging, Replicating Yourself, Hiring Forward, Getting Customers to Buy More, Licensing, Getting Paid by Retainer, Franchising, Creating Certification Programs, and Buying Competitors.
- DO create your Business Blueprint to market more effectively to your customer.
- DO drive cash flow with your customers with creative methods such as being a connector and showing appreciation.
- DON'T ever undervalue your products or services.

Alliance of the Team

Focus on the who, *not the* how. *You can always find someone to do it for you. Successful entrepreneurs make offers and deals and build* how *teams.*
—Excerpt from my interview with Mike Koenigs, serial entrepreneur, bestselling author, and speaker. To watch my full interview with Mike Koenigs, go to: www.ScaleorFail.com/bonus.

Christine's Story of Letting Go and Leading

When I began working with Christine, she had already been in business for 10 years with her husband, Alex. They run a cold-storage construction company, A-N-C Cold Storage, Inc., that builds cold-storage facilities for companies like Bon Appetit Bakery and Golden State Foods. They prided themselves on their great work, but their business had been at a standstill for several years. When they started working with me, I saw they had tremendous potential for growth, but were stymying the possibilities by trying to control all of their company's daily operations. Everything that came in or out of their business had to pass the "Christine approval test," which became a huge bottleneck for projects and created significant frustration for her and her team.

Christine and Alex were trying to grow their organization from entrepreneur to enterprise utilizing the same practices and procedures as the ones they had used from Day One. They were on an endless hamster wheel working so hard to get everything done so that their business would not implode. This is an impossible, endless task and they had hit their ceiling of growth by operating in this manner.

As you grow your company, everything must evolve. The company you start with will not be the same one you grow with.

Christine and Alex's dilemma is a common roadblock that stunts the growth of so many small businesses. No one likes giving up control for fear of mistakes, balls dropped – or, even worse, money slipping through the cracks. The irony is that, by keeping an iron fist on every project and task in your company, you are doomed to remain small and are choking every possibility for growth. You are sending a message to your team that you don't trust them, so they don't step up and own their projects. You waste so much of your precious CEO time running around in the business instead of building a team of experts who can help you let go and free you up so you can scale. To experience big profit leaps and build the enterprise you have been working toward, you must make time to work on your business strategies and create valuable relationships that can open doors for your business and ultimately sustain a more self-managed company. Christine and Alex had an immense fear of hiring the team members they needed for project management, marketing, and sales. However, with the right team players, Christine's business would grow wings and soar.

As we began working together, I helped her build out her infrastructure and her team one new position at a time. Christine stepped up as a powerful leader and a visionary. She established a team that was committed and fired up about the vision for growth, so she could start letting go and trusting that they could handle the work. Within two years, their business grew 667%. They began going after and snagging million-dollar deals because they had the confidence and the authority in their industry to fulfill the projects from beginning to end. She made that shift from micro-manager to becoming the CEO she was always meant to be.

Slip-ups, falls, misses, and collisions are par for the course in trapeze arts and in business, until that magical moment when everything suddenly works together harmoniously. There is a trust that develops and, instead of hanging on too tightly, you let go and allow your team to step up even further. This is the place where everyone is in alignment and finds their flow.

Like the trapeze, you and your team can create poetry in motion, and this chapter shows you how – no safety net necessary. But before you begin, you need to choose your super power.

Choose Your Super Power: The Four Quadrants

Every small business owner is intensely focused on getting new business, finding new clients, and attracting new customers. That is normal and completely acceptable. But, once you've found new business, signed up new clients, and drawn in new clients, there is a whole other side to the equation that needs to be given equal consideration: *Can the business handle all of this new demand?*

I'll bet I know what most of you are thinking: *No problemo. If I have the sales, you bet I can handle the demand!*

Can you really? Are you so sure of this? If your business doubles or triples – which is no doubt what you want it to do – are the support systems in place in your company to be able to handle all that demand?

In a business, there is always the push/pull of making sales versus being able to fulfill the demand of those sales. It's always a fine line, like balancing on a high wire. You work so hard to get the sales. There could be ten deals in the works in various stages. Some fit right in with your current fulfillment processes, whereas others are gigantic and those deals have needs that far exceed your bandwidth.

What happens if you cannot process these orders quickly enough? How are you supposed to manage it all without tipping over the edge one way or the other? Sometimes this feels totally overwhelming. I've been there many times, wondering what would happen if I missed a step. I might be in the shower or in bed at night and have that queasy feeling: *Oh, did I just agree to do that? Are we set up to handle all that new business?*

In order to simplify things and handle the balance between sales and demand, I came up with the Four Quadrants of business. Bear with me as I explain what this all means and how it will apply to your scaling efforts.

You might have as many as 10 divisions in your business, all of which are moving at the same time: Admin, Product Development, Marketing, Sales, Legal, Finance/Accounting, Manufacturing, IT, Fulfillment, and Human Resources. This is overwhelming when you consider how a significant amount of new work will impact each area of your organization.

I simplified all of these aforementioned areas into the Four Quadrants, aka "Super Powers":

1. **Revenue Streams:** This is everything that your company produces, offers, and sells.
2. **Traffic:** This is how you drive business to find your products or services. In other words, *marketing*. It could be online, brick-and-mortar retail, manufacturing, wholesale, and so forth. This super power is all about how you bring customers and clients to your door.
3. **Sales:** This is all about conversion. Many times companies will lump marketing and sales together. The truth is, they are two distinct aspects of your business. One drives the business to you, while the other converts it into a sale. This is a very important delineation because you might be spending a lot of money on marketing and driving traffic, but you're not getting the conversion that warranted all of that expense. In the reverse, it's possible you are getting plenty of conversion, but don't have enough leads coming to your door. Both are equally as important.
4. **Operations:** This area consists of anything to do with your team, the systems that support them, and finance.

Now that we've condensed 10 areas into 4, ask yourself, "Which one of those four is my personal Super Power?" and fill out the 4 Super Pros of Business Success chart (Figure 4.1). This is unbelievably important, so take a moment to think about it. Are you, the founder of the company, strong or expert in Revenue Streams, Traffic, Sales, or Operations? Where do you truly shine? Are you working on areas that are not your strength? Why? You know the saying, "Play toward your strengths."

It's time to find experts who can work in the areas where you are not at your top strength.

Here's the importance of choosing a Super Power. Picture a trapeze: It has cables on all four sides. Every one of those cables

PINNACLE GLOBAL NETWORK®
THE WORLD LEADER IN SCALING BUSINESSES

4 SUPER PROS of Business Success

Revenue Streams Pro Products and Services

Who

Strategies

Traffic Pro Driving leads to your business

Who

Strategies

Sales Pro Conversion of buyers & repeat buyers

Who

Strategies

Operations Pro Managing people, projects, tech, customer support, finances

Who

Strategies

© Allison Maslan International

Figure 4.1: Identifying the Four Super Powers and people who excel at them.

is essential because if one becomes loose, the whole thing might come tumbling down.

The same thing can happen in your business. You need all four areas of your company supported, directed, and humming along smoothly. But, if you think about it, most companies have only one or two of the four quadrants running well. Do you wonder why your business isn't soaring, or even feels like it is sinking at times?

If your business isn't flourishing, it probably means you have a missing, broken, or wobbly cable or two – that is, your weak quadrants. In all likelihood, those are not *your* super strengths or passion areas, either.

I'm going to give you some wonderful news: You only have to focus on the quadrant or two in which you and your company excel. Why should you only play to your strengths? Your strengths are your *gifts* – and where you will find your greatest happiness and success. When you can play to your strengths, you become more focused and engaged. You can experience higher levels of innovation and creativity, instead of ripping your hair out working on your weaknesses.

Which quadrant of your company will it be – Revenue Streams, Traffic, Sales, or Operations? Which one is your Super Power? I am granting you full permission to devote your energy and attention to it. It's not that you don't care about the other areas or that they aren't important. Immerse yourself in the parts of the business that are flying in the air with finesse and grace (and a flip or two). This is the fun part of the business, isn't it? Enjoy it! Flaunt it!

I have not forgotten the missing, broken, or wobbly quadrants. They need repair and improvements, or you know what will happen: everything will come crashing down.

Not only do I give you permission to spend all of your time and energy on your Super Power(s), I also grant you the authority to hire the best people to manage the weak parts of the business. Once again I'm psychic and I know what you are thinking: *Oh, I'd love to hire Debbie, but I really can't afford the best people.*

Here's the thing: If you recruit strong talent to manage the other three areas, you become free to focus on your Super Power. Suppose, for example, Traffic is a weak quadrant for your company. Try as you might, you don't have the knowledge or skillset to increase the number of customers being attracted to your product or service. You hire a Senior VP of Marketing who is the uber maestro of driving online traffic. She costs a fortune, but within two months she has increased traffic to your company by 5%. After six months, it's up 30%. In a year, it's up 50%. This means your Sales quadrant has more leads to convert – which means mega-revenue!

You aren't completely off the hook. If your Super Power is Sales and you are responsible for driving most of the revenue in your company, you will have so much pressure to keep the cash coming in that you will not have time to work on your Big Picture Vision, relationship building, and strategy. Ultimately, you will need to replicate everything you know about sales so you can replace yourself. Train someone else on your gift so that you can step back. Otherwise, you will get lost in the weeds.

These are two of the most liberating things you will ever do with your business: (1) Hiring experts in your company to handle the three weak areas and (2) Honing in on your Super Power quadrant, so you can work toward replicating yourself. Then you can hand that quadrant over as well and ultimately take that responsibility off your plate. By following these simple practices, you will have four Super Powers and the most fail-proof business in your industry. This is how you build a self-managed company. How freeing is that!

Hiring Will Free You from the Weeds to the Trees

I believe one of the top three roadblocks to growth for business owners is their fear of spending money on hiring new employees. Studies have shown that business owners who hire within the first six months of business jump to seven figures much faster than those that don't.

If you're spending time doing work that can be done by someone else for $15 to $20 per hour, you are losing money! Think about it this way: While you think you are saving this money by doing the job yourself, you are actually losing up to $2,000 in opportunity costs in new business you could have initiated in that time. In order to scale, you must be willing to commit fully to taking those scary leaps and hiring people. Otherwise, your business dreams will never be fully realized.

It's not as if you will always have a chunk of money sitting in your bank account waiting to be spent on employees. That is usually not the case. However, the sooner you hire, the sooner your bank account balance will rise. You just need a few months to cover their salary; after that, they will pay for themselves and even more.

In his early days as an entrepreneur, Richard Branson was known to compel new employees to work for him for less money by communicating his impassioned vision. This is how he was able to grow Virgin so quickly.

So many of my clients have fears of leveraging growth by building a team. Once they've done it, however, I always hear: "Why didn't I do this a long time ago? I can't imagine working without them!" Hiring will shift you from the weeds to the trees so you can stay focused on your Big Picture Vision.

If payroll taxes are a concern, you can always start by hiring freelance, virtual, or part-time independent contractors and/or paid interns. My rule of thumb is that, once you are paying your freelancers more than it would cost to hire a full-time employee, it's time to make the shift. At that point, hire the freelancers full-time or recruit people for those in-house roles.

There are myriad benefits of having full-time employees versus supporting freelancers or independent contractors, even outside of cost. Primarily, you have people working for you who are committed to your company, your products or services, and the team's goals. They are *vested*.

Additionally, freelancers work for many other clients and are well within their rights to pick and choose what they work on and in what order of priority. Employees, however, are completely focused on your company's needs and are there when you need them. You can work with them to ensure that the priorities and deadlines are in check. With an employee, you are investing in the long-term training, development, and growth of the individual, whereas a freelancer can stop at any time and then you have to start training from scratch all over again.

Hiring the Right People

> It doesn't make sense to hire smart people and then tell them what to do; we hire smart people so they can tell us what to do.
> —*Steve Jobs, cofounder of Apple, Inc., innovator,*
> *entrepreneur, and business magnate*

In Chapter 3, we covered the importance of *hiring forward* in order to scale your business. It may seem obvious but it needs to be stated that when hiring forward – or hiring anyone – you need to feel 100% confident in your gut that you are bringing in the right person for the right position. Even when taking into account all the advice and steps to follow in this book, the power of intuition trumps everything. Some candidates may seem like superstars on paper, but you may be sensing that something doesn't feel right. You can't put your finger on why, but the dots aren't connecting between this candidate and your open position. Listen and pay attention to clues that are floating in the air, as they can potentially save you many heartaches and thousands of dollars.

The fact is, the cost of hiring and onboarding the wrong person could cost you between 6 and 15 times that individual's annual salary. This may sound like an exaggeration, but it's not – and misfire hires happen all the time. Think about the amount of the time and energy you spend searching for candidates, creating job descriptions, writing ads, plowing through resumes, interviewing candidates, checking references, negotiating terms, and running background checks – all before the new hire starts on Day One! Then the real work begins with the training processes, which chew up a lot of time. You are investing in the future of this new employee and it can take weeks, if not months, to get him or her fully onboard and acclimated. However, you want to start seeing results quickly so you can begin recouping your investment.

It should go without saying that your recruiting process needs to be spot-on or else you'll have a revolving door of employees and will have wasted a ton of money, time, and energy.

Finding the Perfect Fit

When I'm searching for new employees, I seek to "hire where the fish are" – meaning, I try to get referrals from my team members and even clients. Since the people I approach are solid employees and enjoy working for my company, chances are pretty good they can identify someone who has the skills and is the right cultural fit.

Trade shows can be an excellent venue for finding recruits. If you need somebody in technology, go to a technology tradeshow. If you need somebody in the health arena, go to a health tradeshow. Meet the people in their environments where you can see them in action.

It also goes without saying that all bets are off when it comes to hiring talent from other companies. It happens all the time in every industry and you shouldn't feel the least bit guilty about it.

Now, you may be asking: "Don't you care about other companies doing the same and poaching from you?" Not at all. My feeling is that, if I have employees who are looking around and considering working for a different company, those individuals are not committed to my company's vision. Of course, I have to take ownership and try to understand why they are looking elsewhere. I always address the situation with one-on-one conversations, so that I have a better understanding of their discontent and can see if there is anything I can do to improve my employee relations. Either way, I don't want somebody on my team who doesn't want to be there – and neither do you. By the same token, trying to save the position by offering more money is a temporary fix, at best. Statistics show that employees generally leave within six months of turning down an offer from another company. If a person's heart isn't in his work, he will probably end up leaving on his own anyway.

Once I've pared down the number of qualified candidates to five or fewer, I always have my team start with a surprise phone call. You can tell so much about someone by the way he answers the phone, handles the "out-of-the-blue" moment, and demonstrates enthusiasm for the position. Of course, you must take into account that the candidate may be in the middle of something important. Even so, catching someone in the midst of "real life" can often reveal more than when he is prepared and ready. You want to see how a candidate acts when he is *not* prepared. The rule of thumb is that I don't want to waste my time or theirs, and this process helps me weed out many candidates without having to go through the process of a formal interview in the office.

Third Time Is a Charm in Hiring

Once the candidates pass the first couple of hurdles, apply the Rule of Three. This consists of at least three good candidates and three interviews in three locations by three different people.

You learn a great deal about a candidate when she is required to interview at least three times – not only by what she says, but what she does. How much effort is she putting into the process? Is she persistent? Is she willing to take the extra steps necessary to prove her skills – even if it means taking a test or assessment and/or providing examples of their talents? Does she follow up with a call and a thank-you letter or card? Does she show up on time on all three occasions? Is she consistently dressing in a way that fits your brand? Does she hold the door open for others? Does she treat others with kindness? A good question to ask yourself is, "Could you see yourself sitting next to this person on an international flight?"

Studying a candidate's behaviors reveals a great deal more than asking basic interview questions. When someone goes on three interviews, she may say something inconsistent or suspicious between meetings. Or, she may lose the "character" she was playing by the third visit.

> When I'm interviewing candidates, I look for people who ask questions. A lot of questions. Deep questions about whether they can grow these businesses.
>
> At least in my industry, I've found that the people are coming from large beverage and food companies. They have baked-in ideas about what can and can't be done. It's almost harder to undo those things because they think, "Well, I've worked for a company that's one hundred years old."
>
> This is what I say to that: "Well, that's great. But you guys haven't innovated in the last 50 years, at least."
>
> —*Excerpt from my interview with Kara Goldin, CEO and Founder of Hint, Inc. For the full interview, go to: www.ScaleorFail.com/bonus.*

Desperate hiring leads to hiring the wrong fit almost every time. People do their best to show up and display their best selves. When you hire on the spot, you miss all of the important warning signs about the person you might be welcoming into your company culture – hopefully for many years to come. Isn't that worth taking the time to make sure she is truly the right fit?

This is why you need time to dig deeply to determine if the person you are meeting with is the same person who will show up to work at your company.

If you don't have anyone else to interview a candidate, ask your significant other or a client or friend. Someone who knows you and your needs and won't be swayed by a candidate who says all the right things, yet has nothing to back up these claims. Ask your co-interviewers to have their eyes open for potential red flags.

Several years ago, I placed an ad to hire an in-house public relations manager. I was contacted on LinkedIn by a woman who had years of experience in the television world and who, on the surface, appeared extremely professional and knowledgeable. During her interviews, she said all the right things regarding her dedication, skills, passion, and approach to overcoming adversity. I became excited to add her to our team. On Day One of her employment, I overheard her say the word "overwhelmed" at least three times. (Let me repeat: *This was only the first day!* Not a good sign...) Over the coming months I realized that she could not handle taking on more than one task at a time and everything needed to be repeatedly explained in great detail. She did possess one solid skill: a knack for sales. Prospects would walk into the door and she could close a sale with them like nobody's business. As a business owner, this is always a big plus and, honestly, the main reason I didn't let her go, despite my reservations.

Soon enough, my other employees began complaining about her tirades and meltdowns. She even burst into my office one day to inform me that three of our team members were out to get her.

An important question occurred to me: *Who is the common denominator here?*

I let her go the next day and proceeded to hear all kinds of complaints from my staff about her that they had suppressed. (In most cases, employees won't tell you what is really going on until the person is gone.) Even though she was great in sales, we were losing productivity and it was wearing down the team. The lesson: Dig deeply in your interviews and do trial periods whenever possible. One wrong cultural fit can wreak havoc upon your business.

> Be willing to destroy anything that is not excellent.
> —*Joe Polish, marketing authority, entrepreneur, and innovator*

How Do You Know If You Have the Right Team?

Knowing whether you have the right team isn't just about how well your company is doing financially (although that is extremely important). This is the question you need to ask yourself: *Are you happy when you go to work?* You should be excited to be around the people you hired. If you're not, then something's wrong. These are some good telltale signs you have the right people on board:

- You want to hang out with them.
- You want to take them to dinner.
- You would have fun in a long car ride with them.
- You enjoy business trips with them.
- You would rehire them again if need be.

Hire Slowly, Fire Fast

As brutal as the above saying might sound, you can't afford not to abide by it. If an employee isn't a good fit, it's not fair for either of you to keep him or her on your team. It's no different than being in an intimate relationship with someone you are no longer interested in, but not breaking up with him because you feel bad and don't want to hurt his feelings. To me, that's selfish and dishonest because you're pretending to be interested and wasting his time and affection. You are also keeping him from finding a great relationship. In business and in relationships, a breakup might be painful at that moment, but ripping off the Band-Aid gives them an opportunity to find a better fit and removes the bottleneck in your business.

Firing: It's Just Business

When I was little and went to my dad's office, I saw many things that inspired me later in life when I started my own business. The one thing I had a tough time reconciling was when my dad let people go. It upset me to see an employee walk out of his office with tears in his or her eyes. I would think, *Oh my God. He is the meanest dad ever. How could he ever do that to this poor person?*

Now, having had to let several people go over the years in my own businesses, I understand the plain truth: Not everyone is going to be a fit. The surprising thing is, although letting someone go is my least favorite business activity to do, the employee and I normally part ways on good terms. We feel like lessons have been learned on both sides, drawing the mutual conclusion that the position had not been heading in the right direction for some time, in spite of all our efforts to try to make it work.

But the sooner you replace an underperforming employee with someone who is a better fit, the sooner you can get your business on track and step things up a notch. Chances are, if you had issues with the employee, so did the rest of your staff, who may have been covering up for that person all along. You find out so much about the troubled or wrong-fit employee after she leaves. The rest of your team may even be relieved, if not grateful, that you are starting fresh with someone new.

Yes, it may come across as harsh, but the fact is that the devoted people who helped you get your company off the ground are not necessarily the same employees who have the abilities needed to bring your company to the next level. They may be great at starting things out, but then when the organization becomes rote and systematic, they might not be knowledgeable enough to keep up with the changes and developments necessary for the business to grow. There is also the chance that they become stuck in their boxes and are unwilling to do what is necessary out of fear of change or of the unknown. When employees hold back, it can be dangerous for a company's growth.

The Vibe of Your Tribe

In order to be a successful leader, you must create a rad company culture (meaning "radically awesome"). I call this the *vibe of your tribe*. It will drive the happiness of your team, your clients, and even you. People want to work for and with companies that have a strong vibe.

My team is always number one. I believe in them, take care of them, and show my appreciation to them every day. If they are happy, feel like they are well treated and respected, and enjoy being part of a cool company culture, they will try to take even better care of our customers.

> Customers will never love a company until the employees love it first.
>
> —*Simon Sinek, bestselling author, motivational speaker, and marketing consultant*

Sometimes you may have the right people, but they are in the wrong positions. You may have a diamond in the rough who is not displaying her true talents, perhaps because she hasn't had the opportunity to do so. Discover what's unique about every person on your team and capitalize on these skills. There is nothing more motivating to an employee than providing an outlet at work for his or her talents and passion to shine. One way to do this is to take the time to meet with your key team members and ask them their personal dreams and goals. Then do what you can to help them realize these dreams.

My creative director has been with me now going on six years. Besides working for me, he is an extremely talented film-maker. He has had a dream to create his own film for years. When he launched a kick-starter campaign to raise funds to produce a mystery movie, I immediately gave a large donation to help with his efforts. When you hold people back from following their hearts, they become disengaged and leave anyway. When they see you care, the game changes and the relationship changes. Give with a purpose. Support their dreams and they will support yours.

Let the Meetings Begin!

One way that I strengthen the alliance with my team is by having a standing weekly meeting with my entire coaching team at Pinnacle Global Network. We have not missed a meeting in the past three years and it has made a tremendous impact on our connection and comradery as a team. Rather than making it a stale meeting about "projects," the call is a brainstorm session about one thing: *our clients*. We are solely focused on navigating the challenges our clients are facing. We discuss ways to solve their problems and capitalize on opportunities. No one on the team feels as if he or she is flying solo. The team becomes excited and productive in this collaborative environment while merging their collective brainpower and creativity to search for solutions. Who benefits the most from this interaction? The clients, of course, who reap the rewards of working with an engaged and elevated team.

We also hold a weekly marketing, administration, and sales meeting. By sticking to these weekly commitments, my team feels supported, they know what needs to get done, and it keeps the momentum of our company going. In the early days, I was always changing the meeting dates and times due to my schedule, and I realized that this was causing confusion and unrest on our team. Our communication was erratic, which caused them to feel confused about what was expected of them. The problem was me – the CEO – and – I had to own that. I had to make the commitment to show up and stick to it. This one practice has made a massive difference in their trust in me, their ability to meet project deadlines, and their overall happiness.

In addition, you want to schedule monthly, quarterly, and annual meetings to review progress toward achieving goals and the Big Picture Vision. These meetings are a good opportunity to do a temperature take of individuals, teams, and the company as a whole while also sharing in everyone's successes. If things are slipping, it's also the right forum to bring those issues out into the light before it's too late and make some course corrections. When you take the full day with your team and hold a planning meeting for the entire year ahead, you can create substantial growth, solve pressing issues, and get the team excited about what is to come.

You also take pressure off your own shoulders because, if you allow them to, your employees will begin to take ownership of their roles. Your team is smart and creative. Allow them to share their ideas and solutions. If you let them, they just might blow you away! This is how you grow. Then follow up with all-day quarterly team meetings to make sure you are meeting your goals and staying on top of your yearly objectives.

On the Fly with Your Virtual Teams

In today's high-tech business climate, many companies have found ways to create collaborative team alliances that include offsite people who communicate virtually. Video conferencing, phone conferencing, texting, IM systems, VPNs, shared servers and, of course, regular email have become the norm to help employees communicate with each other and share, transmit, and review each other's work.

Managing virtual employees entails a few additional challenges because those individuals can get left out of hallway conversations and decisions made on the fly in the office when they can't be reached. These employees can't be held accountable for things they weren't told. Your offsite team needs to feel elevated, too, so it's extra important that you (or a designated employee) keep them in the communication loop as things happen. Offsite employees may not be visible all the time, but remember that they are a crucial part of your company's success.

Most important, you must ensure that they buy into your Big Picture Vision and feel connected to it at all times. One way to do so is to have what I call "Happy Hour Virtual Parties" with your entire team (in-house and virtual people all together). This is something like a daily huddle (some companies refer to it as an "All Hands" meeting), except that it's done by video conferencing.

One of my clients created a daily practice that is aptly named "Tuck-Ins." This is where all employees get a check-in call at the end of the day. Typically, there is no agenda; it's just a check-in to see how their days went and to say "have a good night." It also gives the offsite employees a chance to raise critical issues and questions that otherwise might not have been aired. In the early days of his business, Marshall personally made all of the calls. Now his service managers do them. His team feels taken care of and appreciated and all loose ends are handled.

If you have offsite employees, try to implement end-of-day "Tuck-Ins" with them. You'll find that you can go to bed without worrying that anyone on your team has "bed bugs"!

Your Role as Leader of Your Company, Your Team, and Your Culture

Often the company CEO feels like he or she is carrying all of the weight of the business on his or her shoulders. "Will I meet our financial needs? Will we get the deal? Will the projects get done? Will the clients be happy?" It's impossible for anyone to scale with such a heavy burden. There is the old cliché of the business owner who proudly "wears all of the hats" in the organization, but this is an absurd concept. No one is expected to know how to perform every single job function in an organization, and there is no way any individual can juggle them all at the same time and still do them well – just as in Christine's case in the opening story of this chapter.

The CEO's central tasks are these four areas: create and establish the Big Picture Vision; identify what needs to get done; bring the right people aboard to run the business; and provide the support, environment, and tools to make it all happen. Then the CEO needs to get out of everyone's way.

Our job as business owners is *not* to know how to do everything. Stop thinking you have to do so much by yourself. You started the business. You may even have the capability to continue to run some or most of it. But any great CEO recognizes that, in order to grow, he or she must accept that this role is changing and learn to delegate – even when the tasks seem familiar or comfortable, and he has a perception that only he can do the job up to his high standards.

As the CEO, you are the *who* (hiring), the *what* (creating the Big Picture Vision), the *where* (establishing the future business direction), the *when* (targeting dates for big picture goals), and the *why* (giving your team purpose behind the Vision) person.

> We treat our people like royalty. If you honor and serve the people who work for you, they will honor and serve you.
> —*Mary Kay Ash, founder, Mary Kay Ash Cosmetics, Inc.*

What vital question word is missing from the above? The *how.* You should never be doing the *how* – executing the details yourself – which means you need to surround yourself with amazing *how* people. You're the visionary: You need to hire and retain the best *how* people – the talented *doers and experts* – who, in essence, are the operational implementers. They are being paid to carry heavy loads so you don't have to. Why would you recruit them in the first place and continue to pay their salaries if you're doing their jobs for them? Isn't that a waste of money and their time (as well as being somewhat demoralizing to them?). It's so easy to say, "This will only take me five minutes. I'll just do it." Yes, it is only five minutes – *over and over again*. You think these tasks are quick, but they add up to a tremendous amount of lost time – which ultimately costs you a ton of revenue.

Jan Arnold is the cofounder of Creative Nail Design (CND) who revolutionized the nail industry with Shellac. She has steered CND for 29 years, selling it to Revlon for $660 million in 2013. Jan still carries the torch for her brand with an undying passion that extends to her entire team. She is one of the kindest and most creative CEOs I have ever met. I had the pleasure of interviewing Jan recently at one of my events.[1]

For me it's all about finding the right people that are passionate and have a love for the brand. You have to empower them to own whatever you are doing. If I have a great idea, I go to the people I trust and empower them to carry a torch for the company, then they will take it to the next level. If I make it a 5, they will make it a 10. My idea is the seed that must blossom. My job is to sell the moon. If I can get them to believe it is there, and it can be ours, that is my job. Once they own it, we can do anything.

—*Excerpt from my interview with Jan Arnold, cofounder of Creative Nail Design. Watch the full interview at: www.ScaleorFaleBook.com/bonus.*

Your employees are the people who are going to help you get from *here* to *there*. You need to trust in their abilities and that they're going to figure out the *how*. It's just like parenting. If you

---

[1] www.nailsmag.com/article/97137/revlon-buys-back-cnd-parent-company-colomerwww.nailsmag.com/article/116913/a-day-at-cnd

are always jumping in to be the hero instead of enabling your children to fall, learn, get up and apply the lesson on their own, they won't be self-sufficient and have the confidence to do it the next time without you. As a result, they could remain stuck for years to come.

Instead of this outcome, try empowering them with responsibility. When you step away from the business, let them know you trust them to hold down the fort. Point out all the positives they handled when you return. The more you focus on what they are achieving without your micro-management, the more responsibility they will want to take on and the more they will achieve.

Practice becoming a master delegator. Keep focusing on letting go of the top three things that take up most of your time. This is a tough one to follow through on because you must let go of the way you've been doing things and handle them differently. Habits die hard, if you let them. Practice letting go of things you are doing just because "that is what you have always done." Examine new ways of approaching a project, practice, or problem. Guess what is on the other side? Scaling and freedom.

The flipside of this is that sometimes the CEO gets frustrated because her people become *too operational*. They don't get the CEO or her new ideas right away, if at all. That's perfectly okay! A CEO is the visionary who is thinking ahead to the future – perhaps even light years ahead of the team. You may become passionate about new ideas that are derailed and shot down by tactical and practical people such as your COO, your CFO, or your accountant. You want them to see the unseen – the magic that lies ahead of them. However, operational people tend to *see what is*. A good CEO is looking to shake things up, experiment, take calculated risks, and innovate. Your operational team needs to get behind you and figure out a way to make it happen. They also need to advise you when you could be heading down a wrong path, or when a potential problem is brewing in your company. It is important to weigh all sides – and then you must decide.

You ultimately want your team to get on board with your vision. If they are passionate and excited about what you are all creating, there is no end to what they can do. Naturally, you want them to feel comfortable enough to tell you if they see any problems and, when this occurs, you must listen. Ultimately, however, once you give the go-ahead, they must buy in to your ideas, direction, and overall vision and figure out the execution part to the best of their ability. If they don't, they will stop your energetic flow of creativity and curiosity, and you may find yourself losing passion, personal inspiration, and love for your business.

Creating the Pinnacle Experience

In my company, we have a phrase, "the Pinnacle Experience," which means that we all work together to go above and beyond for our clients to create a rewarding and fulfilling experience for them. Ultimately, customers decide to stay or go based on the experiences they are having. My team works together to come up with creative ideas to surprise and support our clients. For instance, we send glass gratitude balls to our new customers to show our appreciation. We host contests and give away trips to Hawaii and spa weekends. Or, we'll even send them texts to show them how much they are appreciated or to wish with them good luck on a presentation. If my employees thought of their roles as "just a job," then they would not get so involved in sharing their ideas and helping to implement these special extra touches.

Support Your Peeps

Many business owners get frustrated with their employees without realizing that they may be the cause of most of the problems. Either they hired the wrong people for the positions, didn't define their roles clearly, gave too many roles to one person with unclear expectations, didn't train them well, failed to communicate clearly (or enough), or have not created an environment in which people feel safe, heard, and appreciated. The more that employees are moved by your compassion and kindness, the more loyal they will become. When I shared with my father one of the biggest challenges our clients struggle with – finding good employees – he said to me, "This is not true. There are many great people out there. You just need to have patience and train them well."

In my early entrepreneurial days, I had the notion that new employees should know what to do. In other words, they should be able to read my mind. Expecting them to be psychic is nutty and unfair. Take the time and put systems and processes in place to make sure your onboarding and training processes are solid. As you scale, this is crucial for securing good employees and streamlining their assimilation into your organization.

If you want your employees to step up and shine in their roles, give them even longer training that you think is necessary. Have them shadow you or another appropriate person in your company. Instead of recreating the wheel every time, create short videos explaining important processes and procedures and then upload them on the cloud or your server. Have your new employees watch them and send in their takeaways, so you know they are following along and understanding.

If you are training salespeople, an even longer process is recommended. Have them listen in on calls and accompany you on sales meetings. Record their sales calls and provide feedback on them. I recommend this process for at least six months as they are diving into sales. Discuss customer objections and provide opportunities for practicing by role-playing. The more prepared they are, the more your revenue will soar. Make sure you have at least one meeting per week to discuss leads, meetings, and strategies for those prospects in your pipeline. The more accountability you provide within your company, the more successful they will be.

Wherever possible, I try to be as supportive and understanding as possible with my employees. I have always found that, when I demonstrate empathy with a staff member, the individual always returns the favor with even greater commitment to the company. In my early days, I used to walk into the office, say a quick hello, and then scurry into my office and shut the door. This was not because I was being rude; I simply had a lot on my mind and was focused on getting things done. Type A people like myself are highly driven and are always focused on what needs to be done next. I learned early on that this does not work as you seek to build a cohesive and powerful company culture. Stop, breathe, and smell the roses. Take the time to connect with the people who are helping you build your vision. As the years have passed, I realized how much I value this time with my team. It is one of the most fun parts of running a business. Take care of your team and, in turn, they will take care of your business.

According to a 2017 *Forbes* article, 66% of employees said they would leave their companies if they felt underappreciated. That number tilts up to 76% when the Millennial population is polled. This underscores the importance of treating your employees with respect and showing appreciation for their efforts wherever appropriate.

The little things do matter. Take a few minutes out of every day to talk to your people and get to know them. Find out how they're feeling, how their vacations went, and how their kids are. Remember these details for future conversation. By demonstrating interest in them and paying attention, your employees will feel a deeper connection and be even more loyal to you.

Cocreating with Your Team

Not too long ago I invited Robert Richman, the former cultural strategist at Zappos, to speak at one of my Pinnacle Global Network events. He used the phrase *cocreating* when referring to how a leader collaborates with his or her team to work through issues and come up with solutions together.

Many times I've worked with my team to figure out the best way to solve a problem and how we can best support each other. We also hold each other accountable for doing what we say we are going to do. This is cocreating, which is quite different from a leader barking out orders: "Okay, Barry, you need to do A, B, and C. Heather, you need to do D, E, and F. I want it all on my desk tomorrow morning." Cocreating means asking them what they feel is the best way to solve a problem or capitalize on an opportunity.

Employees need to feel like they're part of the creation and the solution. If you want to encourage your team to accomplish something, if you want them to be more passionate and loyal, sit down with them and ask them their opinions and their ideas. *Really listen.* Allow them to show you what they can do. Then watch the magic unfold.

"You Had Me at Hello"

Positivity is contagious and it starts with you right at the top. Your employees take note of everything you do from the first moment you walk in the door in the morning. Are your shoulders slumped? Do you seem frantic or worried? Are you muttering to yourself in anger? Or, are you smiling, saying "Good morning," and starting up casual conversations with people?

> A key ingredient in strong relationships is to develop emotional connections. It's important to always act with integrity in your relationships, to be compassionate, friendly, loyal, and to make sure that you do the right thing and treat your relationships well.
> —*Tony Hsieh, CEO of Zappos, from his book* Delivering Happiness

Whether you realize it or not, you determine the company's frame of mind each and every day. If people see that you are stressed out – even if it's about a personal matter – the office chatter will spread like wildfire. They'll hear it in your tone, read it on your face, and interpret it from your body language. "Did you see Allison today? I've never seen her so worried ... something must be wrong. Maybe we lost a big client? What are we going to do? What if I lose my job?"

Your employees are going to bounce off you and reflect back how you deal with everything. If you are positive about something that is going haywire, they will feel and respond positively, too: "Well, if Allison isn't worried about it, then why should we be?"

No one wants negative doom-and-gloom people on their teams. Excessive negativity and gossip should not be tolerated in your company. If you do find out you have a negative person or gossipmonger in your organization, face it head-on and nip it in the bud. Negativity spreads quickly, and it takes only one Debbie Downer to bring down everyone in the company.

Creating a Culture of Gratitude

What you appreciate *appreciates*. When you express gratitude, you magnify happiness.

My company maintains a daily "gratitude log" on our Facebook page. Every day we post the things we are grateful for. It doesn't have to be a work thing. It could be something we're happy about at home or a fun thing we did on the weekend. We post fun pictures. Someone may even post a message about someone at work she is grateful for.

It's difficult to be fearful or negative when you are posting grateful messages and reading those of others. In fact, you cannot be fearful and grateful at the same time. Within 30 days of starting something like this in your company, you will notice that employee happiness goes up by at least 25%.

Gratitude also means celebrating team wins. In my company, we create a biweekly "rad report" in which we celebrate the success stories and all of the things that went right. This is quite different from other companies I know that focus primarily on postmortems and exploring what went wrong. While it is important to always examine root causes and make improvements when things go awry, celebrating the successes more often will bring a winning vibe to your team.

Many business owners skip ahead way too quickly from their successes before moving on to the next thing. They check the box by saying "thank you" and then ask, "Okay, what are you going to do next?" They believe this keeps employees on their toes. Actually, I am convinced the opposite happens; people feel that their efforts will never be good enough.

As a team, you need to show gratitude by celebrating and rewarding people. Handing out gift cards, dinners out, massages, and so on is great. But also keep in mind that it's not just about giving money and gifts. What are some fun little things that you can do to help people feel appreciated? Here are just a few ideas:

- Order in lunch for everyone from a good local restaurant – or just pizza.
- Bring in ice cream for the team on a hot summer afternoon.
- Set up a company barbecue or picnic.
- Have a food truck day outside your building.
- Go to a fun place after work for Happy Hour.
- Let the team head out earlier than expected before a long holiday weekend.

What creative ideas can you come up with that can help your team feel your gratitude for a job well done?

If you want to have all that you are desiring, you have to drop from your head into your heart, get yourself into a place of love, appreciation, and gratitude and thank God for all the goodness in your life. That is how manifestation happens.

—Excerpt from my interview with Arielle Ford, relationship expert, bestselling author, and speaker. To watch the full interview, go to: www.ScaleorFail.com/bonus.

Barbara Corcoran from *Shark Tank* has shared that one of her biggest secrets to building her real estate empire was throwing crazy and fun parties for her team. She would tell them how to show up dressed in a particular party theme, then whisk them away for an unforgettable evening. If there were any tensions in the company, they melted away as they were all having fun and getting to know one another better outside the pressures of work.

Remember: You set the tone and create the vibe of your workplace. That vibe needs to be creative, supportive, fun, and positive. The team should be able to visualize your business environment and activities as a glittering trapeze act, performing astounding feats while seamlessly working together. If you do this right, your business will reap all of the benefits of a happy and productive workforce and will grow exponentially.

Chapter Summary: You've Got This!

- DO determine your Super Power from among the Four Quadrants and focus on that.
- DO hire the right people and make sure they are in the right jobs.
- DON'T let emotions get in the way of letting go of an underperforming or negative employee.
- DO recognize when your current talent pool isn't capable of taking your company to the next level.
- DO create a company vibe that attracts, engages, and retains the best talent.
- DO elevate your team by surrounding yourself with talented people who know things you don't.
- DON'T ever do the *how* of your business – execution is the team's job, not yours.
- DO create a positive, uplifting, and fun work environment.
- DO reward your team and show gratitude as often as possible.

5

Leading Your Vision

Women must try to do things as men have tried. When they fail, their failure must be but a challenge to others.

—Amelia Earhart, aviator

Leaders Show the Way

When I think of brilliant leaders, the names John F. Kennedy, Nelson Mandela, Margaret Thatcher, Rosa Parks, Martin Luther King Jr., and Golda Meir immediately come to my mind. But I also personally think about my dad in this context. It happens that he had the privilege of meeting Golda Meir in person, and I have a picture of them shaking hands.

I realize I'm probably biased because he was my dad but, objectively speaking, it was plain to everyone that he had some remarkable gifts as a leader. He was especially adept at making people feel comfortable – employees, customers, famous people (like Meir), and even people he didn't know. He led thousands of employees, but treated everyone exactly the same – from the janitors all the way up to his senior staff. Everywhere he went he started up friendly conversations with complete strangers, including taxi drivers. It astounded me how many people would recognize him out of the blue. "How the heck does he know all these people?" I always wondered.

There are some famous stories about celebrities like Tom Hanks (as well as the late Robin Williams), who are reportedly friendly and chatty with pretty much everyone they meet. Hanks, in particular, never seems to have any qualms interacting with fans and has been known to treat them as equals. When not acting, he comes across as just a regular guy. My dad was just like that.

I vividly remember my moment of self-realization. I was so busy dealing with my projects, my top to-do's, and all the other minutiae I had going on. I looked through my office window at my team. They were busy talking among themselves. I had absolutely no idea what they were doing. Likewise, I'm sure they had no idea what I was doing. We were all over the place. Yes, we all had goals and projects, but nothing was integrated. As a result, they seemed lost and confused. I felt frustrated because they weren't getting things done the way I wanted them to. One of my employees even said, "You are like a red Ferrari and we are running so fast trying to keep up with you."

Wow, I thought, *I am truly sucking at being a leader right now.*

I had to admit that the discombobulated culture was my fault. I wasn't leading the team; I was managing and directing them, which is quite different. The team needed more communication, guidance, support, independence, and, most important, inspiration.

At that moment, I made a conscious decision that I was going to shift from being a *boss* to becoming a *leader*. Once I believed I had achieved this over time, I strived to become a *great leader* – which really is a never-ending goal.

Decisions Followed by Perseverance Shape Destinies

When you own your own business, you are the top dog, the head honcho, the big cheese. Everyone looks to you for direction for everything – the big things, the small things, and everything in the middle. It's easy in the beginning to *enjoy* this sense of ultimate command and authority and get accustomed to it. It feels good to be the omnipotent know-it-all who makes every decision with everyone acting subservient to you.

The problem with this is that it just doesn't work – especially when you are scaling. No one succeeds on the trapeze alone, no matter how talented and brilliant you might be. The "dictator leader" is a dinosaur of the distant past.

As I've stated in earlier chapters, you don't know everything and shouldn't have to. If you create a team with a bunch of people who are incapable of making decisions without you, your business will sink fast; or you will have created a ball and chain that you may end up resenting and that will hold you back from scaling.

What will happen when you shift over to a massive scaling initiative, such as acquiring another company, and can't be available to make decisions? Your existing team members will feel paralyzed, helpless, alone, afraid, abandoned, and lost. They need to be trained to become self-sufficient and empowered to make appropriate decisions. You need to draw the line in the sand where your senior employees or team leaders have approval authority – and then you must stand by it, despite temptation.

The Decisions You *Do* Need to Make

As you've surmised by now, a lot of this chapter is intended to steer you away from decisions that others in your business should make. In my view, understanding this point is crucial because it's a common mistake and holds many business owners back from successful scaling efforts.

This is not to say that you should concede every decision. There are, of course, critical ones that you *should* retain. When you are entrenched in your business, sometimes you get so close to it that the lines become blurry with regard to what you should and shouldn't decide. Here is a starter list of the high-level final decisions you should continue to be a part of:

- Direction and vision
- Company organization and department structure
- New positions, hiring, and firing
- New or existing products or services to improve or develop
- Products or services to drop
- Which customers to target and to let go
- Marketing budget
- Anything of a legal nature
- Office selection
- Annual revenue and profit targets
- The budget and capital expenses

If decisions you are making don't fit into your own list, you should question why you're still making them. Look at your team and see which people can be empowered to make those lesser decisions and then train them. You can track progress, but try your best not to interfere – even if they make some obvious mistakes in the beginning. You need to give them some room to fail and grow just like you did, and not attack them for doing their best. This is your time to coach, mentor, and ask questions – not to dictate or berate.

When You Decide, the Magic Unfolds

Several years ago, I decided to host my first big event. Up until that point I had led only small workshops, so this was a pretty big step. Creating an event meant that I had to commit to renting an enormous ballroom. It also required that I fill it up with at least 100 people who would also be hotel guests.

Two months or so before the event, I had to face the frightening reality that only 20 people had signed up to attend. If I were unable to fill up those ballroom seats and hotel rooms, I would have been obligated to pay for an entire extra room block. I couldn't cancel the contract because that would have been at least a $20,000 penalty. I became so desperate that I considered putting on a sign and walking around downtown San Diego to sell hotel rooms. I actually had nightmares that I put blow-up dolls in the audience to make it appear that the ballroom was filled.

I was frantic. I shed many tears of fear. My husband hated seeing me in such agony. I remember him saying to me in his helpless state while watching me suffer: "That's it – you're not doing this again."

But I made the decision to move forward, in spite of the gloomy picture and my fear. It was a huge leap for me, but I pressed on.

In a nail-biting frenzy, just a few days prior to the event, we hit the 100 mark on ticket sales. As the event began and I stepped out onto the stage with my stomach in knots, I knew within three seconds that I had made the right decision. I spent the next few days witnessing so many incredible transformations. It was an indescribable experience. On the second day my husband came up to me in tears and said, "Now I understand why you do this work." I knew in my heart that I was on the right path.

Today I fill ballrooms with over 500 people from all over the world. But it all began with that first big deep breath and the decision to persevere, followed by the willingness to face the fear and make the leap. Since then, my business has grown exponentially.

I share my story with you because most leaders are sitting on two or three big decisions at any given time in their lives. They can't or won't bring them to closure because they're too afraid to make a mistake. Being a perfectionist sounds like something nice to strive for, but it's a fool's mission and generally a sign of procrastination. No one makes the right decisions every time. Meanwhile, as leaders sit on decisions, their employees are waiting . . . waiting . . . and waiting. They are suspended in limbo, their progress and growth become immobilized, and everyone ends up frustrated.

In any moment of decision, the best thing you can do is the right thing, the next best thing is the wrong thing, and the worst thing you can do is nothing.
— *Theodore Roosevelt, 26th President of the United States*

Here's the secret: Even if you make a wrong decision, it's still the *right decision* because at least you're *moving forward*. Why, you are probably asking, is it so important to move forward with a decision even if it's the wrong one? From that decision you'll meet somebody, a door will open, or you'll learn something that gives you insight into making the next best decision for your company. Most of all, your team will finally have closure and can move on. They will forgive you for a wrong decision, but they won't forgive you for a decision that took forever to make. While you were struggling to decide, your team was left hanging from the trapeze in midair.

In order to successfully scale, you need to get input from people you trust, weigh your options, be willing to take calculated risks, and then make the decision. Don't "sit" on it, second-guess, or dilute your process by soliciting too many opinions. Just like the saying "Build the plane while you fly it," the best planning comes through action – not in your head. Just do it, or move on.

The Perfect 10 Decision

In her book *10–10–10*, author Suzy Welch describes a rule of decision-making I've found to be extremely useful. Suppose you are struggling to make a decision and are terrified of the consequences should you pick the wrong option. The 10–10–10 rule forces you to think about how you will feel about your decision in the future: 10 minutes later, 10 months later, and even 10 years later. Will it really matter in any of these time frames? Think about decisions you struggled with in the past that felt monumental to make. Do you even think of them at all now? Probably not. This practice helps you see that, in the "big picture," the outcome most likely won't matter anyway.

Thinking about the decision in the future enables you to separate from the emotions of the moment. You can step back, think more clearly, and gain greater perspective and context to how relative this is in the bigger picture. Even if a mistake happens, is it worth all of this time spent agonizing? Probably not.

Listen Up!

In Chapter 4, I advised listening to your team in specific circumstances. The truth of the matter is that a great leader *always listens*. There is an effective technique known as *active listening* in which your role is to make it clear that you are listening by demonstrating good body language and eye contact; allowing the other person to speak without interruption; and, when the individual is done, repeating back what she has said to ensure you heard it right and understood the meaning. If you didn't understand what she said, she will correct you right away; in addition to setting the record straight, you are demonstrating that you were paying attention and care enough to verify her statements.

It's not easy for the head of a company to sit down and shut up in order to let others speak. People who run companies can be commanding and garrulous, and have strong opinions on everything – especially anything regarding their own businesses. To their credit, many sincerely want to help their employees and provide input and offer wisdom; they just go way too far to "help."

Unless advice is specifically requested, keep totally silent. Do not offer opinions or tell you own stories to show you "relate" to them. Chances are, they will think you are too high up the totem pole to relate to them and they will be rubbed the wrong way or offended – even if you have the best of intentions. Sometimes an employee just wants to vent and can figure things out just by sharing her problems with you.

When you are certain the employee is done speaking, these are things you can say:

- Assure him or her that you will keep the discussion just between the two of you, unless the person wants it shared.
- Thank him or her for sharing the information or idea with you.
- Repeat back what the employee said (active listening). Preface it by stating, "I hear what you are saying."

- Emphasize that you "will look into the matter."
- Show interest by asking questions about what the employee said.
- Provide constructive feedback only when asked for it.
- Let the employee know that you are there in the future if he or she ever wants advice, recommendations, or just a sounding board. State that you have an open door and he or she is always welcome.
- Write down as much as you can about what he or she said at the meeting. You don't ever want to draw a blank the next time you meet with the person, as it would be a sign that you weren't really paying attention.
- If an idea is accepted and approved – or she fixes a problem independently – give her credit and recognition for it!

When you show your employees that you are a good listener, you're making that person feel like she is the only one in the universe at that moment. She will trust you enough to come back to you and open up to you more often. Isn't this far better than babbling your opinions and thoughts to everyone all the time? Believe me: This is something I have had to work on over the years. It is not easy to keep silent when you truly care, like I know you do. In the end, your employee will feel heard and will become more committed toward creating success within your company than ever before. When you are truly present and listen, everyone wins. This is another example of leading by example and influence and will create a culture of good listeners.

Yes, You Deserve Success

This may be hard to believe, but many business owners – who seem strong, powerful, and domineering on the surface – don't feel as if they deserve their success or to take their company to the next level. As outrageous as it may seem, they seem to think they were "lucky" to get as far as they have and at some point the luck will run out. In this regard, they feel like they are somehow not worthy; they are "frauds" who will be exposed if they push the envelope too hard.

Essentially, these business owners lack the confidence necessary to carry the weight of scaling. I've seen firsthand what happens with business owners when their businesses grow, but they have overwhelming fear that they can't maintain it, that things will fall apart, and that they will be embarrassed. Sometimes this can create a self-fulfilling prophecy. If the leader loses confidence, the employees also lose confidence, and then things really start to crumble.

> I learned that courage was not the absence of fear but the triumph over it. The brave man is not he who does not feel afraid, but he who conquers that fear.
> — *Nelson Mandela, former President of South Africa*

Leaders must work on their confidence all the time. They have to be able to handle the entrepreneurial rollercoaster: Business shoots up, business plummets, business shoots up again. Simply accepting this fact can help you become a more resilient leader. When the rollercoaster is at the bottom or creaking upward, you know that sooner or later you'll once again be at the top and will come swooping down, doing loop-de-loops, going upside down, swerving on the side, and then doing it all backwards. As Irish poet and playwright Oscar Wilde once quipped, "To expect the unexpected shows a thoroughly modern intellect."

In my view, what constitutes success is how fast you get back up after being knocked down. After getting KO-ed by a failed business deal, the resilient leader doesn't curse, assign blame, or sulk. Rather, she jumps right back up on her feet and asks, "Okay, what are we going to do about it?" Her brain goes straight into solution mode.

Lead with Heart and Character

Every interaction with your employees is an opportunity for you to demonstrate by words, actions, and silence (if you are in listening mode) that you are a great leader. As mentioned in earlier chapters, you should always be looking for opportunities to show appreciation to your employees by praising them, implementing and acknowledging their ideas, rewarding them, and providing recognition. At the same time, you need to serve as coach and mentor and be fair and consistent in your approach.

These are a few good rules of thumb to consider with every employee exchange:

- **Hold them accountable:** If they agree to a deadline, make sure they stick to it. *Inspect what you expect.* If you delegate and don't follow up, you are sending the message that you don't really care.
- **Turn mistakes into a lesson.** When I was younger, my parents went away for the weekend and gave the babysitter their car to use for transportation. She ended up having a fender bender and was terrified to tell my dad. When my parents came home, I remember the babysitter telling my dad what happened. He stood there silently for a moment and then said, "If you could go into the kitchen and get me a Pepsi, we'll call it 'even Steven.'" And that was it! I remember her seeming so relieved. He knew that getting angry would not change the situation.

    If an employee makes a mistake, don't tear into him – but make sure he fesses up to it and works to repair it. Nobody is perfect and he or she will never perform exactly the same way that you would. Embrace everyone's style. If a person gets to 80% of how you would handle it, you've got a winner on your team. Those who take responsibility learn from their errors and do better next time. They will prove to be some of your best leaders as time goes on.

- **Groom other leaders:** Earlier in this chapter we discussed empowering employees to make decisions. If you elevate and train your team to take on increased responsibility and move up the ladder, you will be freed up to do even more innovative things and will have someone to cover for you when you need to be involved elsewhere else. To scale, you need to ultimately replicate yourself, so this is how that process begins. You will also be surrounded by other leaders, which will create a powerful organization and a motivated culture.

- **Stretch your team outside of their comfort zones:** Just as you need to stretch yourself to grow, so does your team. If you want them to help you scale, they must be willing to expand their capabilities and confidence. The only way to do this is to request they do things that are scary or outside of their skill sets. Initially they may say, "No, I don't want to!" Then, if they accept the challenge and go for it, they will experience that over-the-moon sense of accomplishment. As a leader you also stand in the role of mentor, and that is one of the most rewarding parts of scaling your business.

- **Admit your own mistakes:** A great leader is honest and takes responsibility for his or her shortcomings. Nobody's perfect and you need to set a good example.

- **Offer education:** You are the culmination of the five people you surround yourself with most. This also applies to your team! I believe the expression "a rising tide lifts all boats." If you support continuing education for your team, you will elevate your employees and your company as a whole. In my business mentoring company, any team member can request to attend conferences, take courses, and buy books – so long as she presents what she has learned at our next meeting. This way, she is paying attention at the event, getting the full value of it, and inspiring the team with what she shares.

If your team members aren't growing, they will become bored and stagnant. We are all here on this Earth to grow. You must be the leader who gives them the tools to rise up, even if it means some expense and some days when the person will be away from the office.

- **Embrace conflict:** One of the biggest lessons I have had to learn is how to deal with conflict. As the middle child of three children in my family, I was always the peacemaker. I wondered, *Why can't we all just get along?* However, this does not work in business because sometimes there are upsets or communication breakdowns that need to be dealt with immediately. If you sweep it under the rug and don't address the issue head on, then it will grow like a ragweed. I have learned to walk toward the elephant in the room and embrace conflict. By listening intently to a complaint or dealing with a problem sooner rather than later, you can turn an upset person into a raving fan in a moment. You can also make the necessary changes to avoid this issue in the future. Pick up the phone or deal with the conflict in person, never handle it by email or via text.

- **Don't make excuses:** Imagine you have a team member who spent a month writing up a detailed report. He nervously sends it to you and asks for your input. A week goes by . . . two weeks pass . . . three . . . suddenly it turns into months. The employee sends you friendly email reminders: "I don't want to bother you, I know you're super busy . . . but have you had a chance to look at the report I sent you? I could really use your input." Feeling guilty, you write back: "I'm so sorry, John. I've been tied up on the Petersen deal and then you know the shipment came in late . . . now we're into creating next year's budget. I promise, I'll get to it soon." Instead of making excuses that the employee doesn't care about, come clean: "I'm sorry about this, John. I should have gotten to this sooner. This report is important. I'll send you my thoughts by Friday. Thank you for being so patient." Then, guess what? Make sure you write a thoughtful response by Friday!

- **Keep your word no matter what:** When you say you are going to do something to a client or employee, keep your promise and follow through. Nothing creates distrust faster than flaky people. If a problem arises and something is out of your control, then come clean and do everything in your power to make it right. This is one of my company's core values: *Keep your word always.* If we make a promise and then realize that we made a mistake – even if we will lose money or a great deal of time – we keep that promise, regardless. Integrity builds a strong team, trust, and a referral community. Broken promises create a reputation that you don't want following you.
- **Protect your team**: Do not tolerate people being rude or mean-spirited to your employees. If you stand up for them, they will respect your leadership like nobody's business.

A genuine leader is not a searcher for consensus, but a molder of consensus.

— *Martin Luther King Jr., civil rights leader*

Lastly: *Be real. Be genuine. Be authentic.* Give your employees the opportunity to see you as you really are. It's your business, so you don't need to posture or pretend you are someone that you're not. If you are honest and transparent with your team, they will work hard and pay you back in dividends.

In Figure 5.1, answer the 12 questions on your Leadership Assessment Score to see where you stand up as a leader and areas you need to work on most. Remember: being a leader is like life. It is an ever-evolving journey.

PINNACLE GLOBAL NETWORK®
THE WORLD LEADER
IN SCALING BUSINESSES

How is your Leadership Score Racking Up?
(Rank yourself from 1 – 10 and note changes needed)

1 Do you change your mind all of the time and put your team into a tail spin?

1   2   3   4   5   6   7   8   9   10

Notes:_____
_____
_____

2 Are you brainstorming with your team and unknowingly confusing the heck out of them?

1   2   3   4   5   6   7   8   9   10

Notes:_____
_____
_____

3 Are you playing favorites?

1   2   3   4   5   6   7   8   9   10

Notes:_____
_____
_____

4 Are you talking too much instead of asking questions?

1   2   3   4   5   6   7   8   9   10

Notes:_____
_____
_____

5 Do you accept feedback with "Thank You" instead of "Yes, but"?

1   2   3   4   5   6   7   8   9   10

Notes:_____
_____
_____

6 Do you give credit to your team?

1   2   3   4   5   6   7   8   9   10

Notes:_____
_____
_____

© Allison Maslan International

Figure 5.1: Fill out this leadership assessment as honestly as you can to help you become a better leader.

PINNACLE GLOBAL **NETWORK**®
THE WORLD LEADER IN SCALING BUSINESSES

7 Do you give attention like they are the only one in the universe at that moment?

1   2   3   4   5   6   7   8   9   10

Notes:_____
_____
_____

8 Do you make excuses?

1   2   3   4   5   6   7   8   9   10

Notes:_____
_____
_____

9 How much recognition do you give?

1   2   3   4   5   6   7   8   9   10

Notes:_____
_____
_____

10 Do you respond when angry?

1   2   3   4   5   6   7   8   9   10

Notes:_____
_____
_____

11 If team offers you an idea, do you say "Great, it would be even better if..."

1   2   3   4   5   6   7   8   9   10

Notes:_____
_____
_____

12 Do you admit when you are wrong?

1   2   3   4   5   6   7   8   9   10

Notes:_____
_____
_____

© Allison Maslan International

Figure 5.1 (continued): Fill out this leadership assessment as honestly as you can to help you become a better leader.

Chapter Summary: You've Got This!

- DO identify decisions that you can delegate to others and then train them.
- DON'T micromanage employees who have been empowered to make certain decisions.
- DO make quick decisions and then stick to them.
- DO practice being a good listener.
- DON'T presume your team will respond well to your spontaneous ideas, as you may be inadvertently reversing their direction and causing confusion.
- DO try the 10-10-10 rule to help decision-making.
- DO realize that you deserve every ounce of your success – past, present, and future!
- DO strive to be a better leader each and every day: Your scaling efforts depend upon it!
- DO take the Leadership Assessment periodically to check your progress toward being a great leader.

6

Executing the SCALEit Method

Even a small reduction in errors and rework can have a significant impact.
—Abigail Johnson, president and chief executive officer of
Fidelity Investments

How Melissa Systemized Her Business and Scaled to 40 Locations

Melissa Woods is the Chief Business Mentor at Pinnacle Global Network. In the 1980s, Melissa built a company called JW Tumbles, a children's gym. She was excited in the early years, but, as the company created traction and growth, Melissa found herself chained to her business.

As Melissa recalls: "I had a fantasy of driving off to get milk and never coming back. I realized that if I didn't duplicate myself, it would only get worse. No free time, no ability to take a vacation. No ability to expand. One day – and, yes, this really happened – a princess from Saudi Arabia brought her kids to the summer program and said she wanted to build a JW Tumbles in her country.

"This was my wake-up call, as I realized that my business could be replicated and scaled. I hired a paralegal who was great with systems and especially strong at converting the information we fed her into a digestible format. She would ask us questions about how we did things – what we did the moment we came into the gym every morning in preparation for the day, how we cleaned the gym, what cleaning supplies we used and how we used them (i.e., one spray, two sprays, one wipe). This became an exercise that forced us to think about every tiny detail.

"The hardest part was articulating with pen and paper in a directional format how we deal with our clients. It was so natural to us, we did not realize what we did. We took a hard look at the customer experience – from the moment they stepped into our gym to how we said goodbye to them at the end of a class. We were very serious about it. The gym had to be welcoming every moment people were inside it. This required all the senses. Smell: The gym could not smell like a sweaty kid's gym. Sight: Every piece of equipment had to shine with cleanliness. Sound: We were particular about what music we would play prior to classes starting. It had to be uplifting, happy music.

"I was tasked with watching every move my partner made when we were teaching the kids. I took the job very seriously and was able to see the exact methods he used. I was able to dissect the things he did that were innately 'him' and share them with the paralegal. For example, I studied how he greeted a new child and her parents before they arrived for the first complementary first class. He would first loudly say 'Hello' the moment they came in. Then he would walk over and say to both mom and child, 'Hi, I'm Jeff,' shake the mom's hand, and then look at the new child – but without making eye contact. I asked him why he did this and he answered, 'Because if I make eye contact it freaks them out, it's too confrontational.'

"This tiny little thing made a huge difference in a new child's first experience. It went into the operations manual. There were fifty more nuances like this that he did that over a period of several months. I was able to observe and capture them, so we could train employees on this. Later, we used them to train new franchisees.

"Over the years we were able to expand to several locations. We would get the report on how many new kids came to class weekly, and how many converted to students. If there was a gap in sales, I would go to the site and observe how the staff was approaching parents after a class. I realized they were *not* going up to them. They would just let them leave without having a conversation.

"After observing the class one day I went up to each of the four new kids' parents and started up an easy conversation along the lines of: 'Hey, it looks like Jack had a lot of fun. I loved when he had to tell the story to all the kids and the instructor about his dad's golfing.' The parents were so impressed that I had recalled something special her kid had done that they signed up again right then and there.

"By having observed the workers, I realized they did not know what to say to parents after a class. So they never said anything. Once I recognized this, I added a new training – how to talk to parents.

"Founders of businesses often start a business because they are passionate, and good at what they do. The problem is they do not know how to *teach others to be them*. It requires patience and time. It's all well worth it. My company was able to break down everything we did in the customer experience, so that clients could take their kids to any one of our gyms anywhere in the world and have the same exact experience."

As a result of having stepped back to take the time to systemize every aspect of her business, Melissa grew JW Tumbles to 40 locations in five countries.

■ ■ ■

A key component to successful scaling is ensuring that goods and services are delivered systemically. When Melissa made the shift from her old model of being chained to her business to systemizing everything, JW Tumbles was able to replicate, scale, and become successful anywhere in the world.

Systems, processes, and execution are the behind-the-scenes orchestra to scaling a lucrative and sustainable company. For instance, when someone goes to McDonald's to order a hamburger and fries, they can expect a nearly identical experience at any franchise location worldwide. Ray Kroc conceived of his assembly line–influenced production system long before there was enough demand to inspire 35,000 restaurants. Kroc drilled the process down to the most minor specifications, including weight, fat content, diameter, and even the number of pickles in every single burger.

Now that you've developed your Big Picture Vision from Chapter 2 and have outlined the major tasks involved in achieving it, nothing should get in your way of beginning your scaling efforts – except, perhaps, for *execution*. The good news is that execution problems are entirely within your control and fixable.

With that in mind, it's time to take a look at all of your systems and processes and determine where improvements can be made and things that can be streamlined. This chapter is dedicated to helping you and your organization to break through the barriers, ditch unnecessary steps, avoid repeated mistakes, improve ownership and accountability, and allow your workflow to run smoothly. You may think that you are an expert at execution, and you may very well be. But chances are you are clinging to habits and old ways of doing things that hold you back from getting things done in the most efficient and results-oriented ways possible – and you don't even realize it.

In the early days of building your business, the struggles tend to be around cash flow and getting clients in the door. As you scale, the challenges tend to shift around time – as in, there never seems to be enough of it. Therefore, the need to manage your time and make the most of every minute becomes the priority. I have found myself daydreaming about having an eight-day week and what I could do with that extra day. But truth be told, I would just fill it up with more distractions. The key is to maximize the time we have.

Money comes and goes, but time does not. The time period from just a few minutes ago – when you were reading Chapter 5 – is gone. We cannot get back past moments. If you think about spending time like you spend money, you will choose wisely how you cash in every minute. Choose how you want to invest your time moving forward. How can you maximize these moments? Get clear on the purpose of how you are spending your time.

Don't say you don't have enough time. You have exactly the same number of hours per day that were given to Helen Keller, Louis Pasteur, Michelangelo, Mother Teresa, Leonardo da Vinci, Thomas Jefferson, and Albert Einstein.
—*H. Jackson Brown Jr., bestselling author*

Your Day Is a Series of Investments

What do you want your return to be for the time you invest on your business and your life? If you think of getting a return for every action that you take, then you will choose your actions wisely within the time period that you have. For instance, if you spend your time writing a book, what do you want your return to be for investing that time? Would it be business growth – a sense of accomplishment? If you spend an hour at the gym, eat a healthy meal, or spend time with your children, what is your intended outcome for each of these investments? Good health? Feeling fulfilled? If you binge-watch on Netflix, what is your intended return for investing that time?

Looking at your life this way forces you to take a hard look at how you invest your time, your most valuable asset. Learning how to manage your time and inspiring your team to do the same is the underpinning of what it takes to successfully execute the final phase of the SCALEit Method.

Cashing In on Time

What would you do if you had an extra month per year? What would you do with all of that extended free time? Live in your bathing suit on the beach, write your memoir, spend more time with your friends or loved ones, learn how to play the flute, or fly on the trapeze?

I'm about to give you a gift: the ability to start accumulating your bonus month right now. Here's how it works.

Most people waste at least two hours each day by procrastinating, falling into meaningless, time-sucking activities, working on projects that don't move them toward their Big Picture Vision, tinkering around in social media or on the Internet, or failing to grasp the art of saying "No" and setting boundaries.

Do the math. Two hours per day multiplied by 365 days is 730, which equals one month! If you become more productive two extra hours every day for one year, you will be giving yourself the gift of entrepreneurialism – a complete month off whenever you choose. As time goes on and you master the art of focus, time management, and delegation, you will be able to multiply this time off to several months per year.

Focus, Focus, Focus

In business, a brilliant idea is just a fantasy if it stays only in your head. Execution is when you set your strategy in motion and make it happen. It's all about *taking action*.

You are the visionary, the leader, the idea magnet. *Implementation* – well, that's another story. Execution is not always your best friend, but it's the necessary promise – the Yellow Brick Road to reaching your goals. Do you find yourself moving forward on a task, distracted by another, then get excited as you see something else of interest out of the corner of your eye?

This compulsion, which I call "shiny object syndrome," refers to how some people chase after the newest shiny object within view and forget all about the last one they pursued with exuberance. When entrepreneurs experience "shiny object syndrome," they are exhibiting signs of EADD: Entrepreneurial Attention Deficit Disorder. (This is neither a clinical term nor a diagnosis … at least not yet!)

The fact is, it takes five times as long to get something done when you repeatedly stop and start to do other things. I'm not referring to quick coffee or bathroom breaks or a head-clearing walk, which are necessary and beneficial, but latching onto doing another task while in the middle of something else. Why does it take so long to complete the original task when you return to it? Because it always takes time for your brain to refocus. It's like reading the same sentence over and over in a book, but not really processing it. How wonderful would it feel to dive in fully and get your projects completed in one half or even a quarter of the time? This alone would be life changing!

Perfection is a massive block to most creative types. Remember, get it done and then perfect it along the way. Version 1.0 will open the doors. Then allow Version 2.0 and beyond to evolve and change from the clues and feedback you receive from your market.

Let's focus and get it done!

The Three Ps of Planning

I was a single parent for 12 years. Out of necessity, I learned how to glean the most out of every moment to be able to care for my daughter and run my companies at the same time. I got into the habit of working late after she went to bed at night, so I could be present with her after I picked her up from school. That worked fine for a while, until I realized that if I completed this work during the day – while she was at school – I would be more relaxed when she was home, get a much-needed night of sleep, and feel even more energized the next day. Out of personal necessity, I developed a process to help me stay in the productive zone during the day, so I could be focused on my daughter in the evenings.

When I began mentoring other CEOs, I realized this two-step process could be translated to help them manage their time and, ultimately, their success. The goal for you is to maximize your hours for the things that really fascinate you, lift you up, move the needle forward, and grow your business, while at the same time freeing up your mind so you don't burn out. Plain and simple, this process helps you get more done faster, so you can take charge of your time and your life.

Step 1. **Three Ps of Planning**: Organize your days by working on similar types of activities to keep you in the flow.

Step 2. **Mile Steps and Mini Feats**: Break down your projects into small steps to combat procrastination and complete them faster.

First, divide up your week into three types of days so you can be deliberate in optimizing your activities. The *Three Ps* – Prep Days, Pinnacle Days, and Play Days – help you streamline your days, keep you focused, and help you to get more done in less time.

Prep Days

Prep Days are the days to get your projects done with all the quiet and focused time that you need. For instance, you might need Prep Days to research, create presentations, develop your ideas, write a book, make calls, and perform other essential tasks. I generally take these days at home, or somewhere away from the office where I can think, write, read, and create without interruptions or distractions.

When I have a project deadline, I mark the date on my calendar and reverse engineer the number of Prep Days I require to get the project done. This way I can meet my deadline without stressing out and facing a mad rush. In fact, I am on a Prep Day now as I write this book!

When you get into the creative zone, you want to be able to stay there until you are finished, minus the distractions or the feeling that you should be doing something else. Prep Days allow this to happen.

Pinnacle Days

Pinnacle Days are time spent being "visible." You are "on" with everyone. You brainstorm with your team, meet with new clients and vendors, attend events, represent your brand, sell, interview candidates, present on stage (if that's something you do), or speak to a group outside your organization. I generally have several Prep Days to prepare for big Pinnacle Days, such as leading one of our Pinnacle Global Network Mastermind events. By organizing these activities together rather than spreading them throughout your week, you are able to stay in your outward communicative energy instead of fluctuating on and off all the time. (You also save on wardrobe changes!)

In the early days of my business career, I used to become nervous about presenting on stage, making a sales presentation, or being on camera. I was terrified of forgetting what I was going to say and making a fool of myself. In one early speech I tried so hard to be a powerful speaker that I was failing miserably. I looked up and saw my husband's head in his hands as if to say, "I love you honey, but this is awful. Be yourself!"

After years of speaking, hosting events, and producing my online show, *Allie & You: The Business Success and Lifestyle Show*, which is now a podcast on iTunes, and pushing through that fear, the nervousness eventually disappeared. I finally realized that being "on" is not about performing or trying to be seen in a certain light; this only created anxiety and dread. It is about being your authentic self, just *you being you*. When you can embrace "being you" and speak from the heart, people will be drawn to what you have to say – whether you are leading your team or an audience. If you make a mistake, the people who are in your camp will not judge you. In fact, they will probably love you more … because you are being human.

Play Days

Play Days are allotted for fun time, down time, and rejuvenation time only – where you unplug and go completely off the grid. Yes, this is so important! It's not goofing around for the sake of avoiding work and interactions. Surprisingly, the goal for a CEO is to have as many Play Days as possible while continuing to reach her business goals.

For most business owners, Play Days are usually the most difficult of the Three P's for business owners to embrace. For driven people who have business on their minds seven days a week, it's hard to let go and do something fun without feeling guilty. But *play* is absolutely necessary. In fact, studies show that Fortune 500 CEOs who took more vacation days experience significantly more growth in their businesses. How could that be? Because the most creative breakthroughs do not come when you are pounding away on your computer. They happen when you are relaxed and having fun – away from the office with space to think.

Nine years ago, my friend Joe Stumpf, CEO of By Referral Only, and I were enjoying lunch at the Lotus Café in Encinitas, California, when he started brainstorming with me a new format for my coaching business. He mapped the entire business model on a napkin and the rest is history. This became the birth of my Business Mentoring and Mastermind, Pinnacle Global Network. I launched PGN six months later. This moment was a complete turning point for my life as I shifted from running companies to helping others build their dreams. It has been so incredibly rewarding, and I have never looked back. Had we not taken a break from work and connected on that Play Day, I have no idea what I would be doing right now.

For the past 18 years, I have taken weekly Play Days to drive from San Diego to Los Angeles to train on the flying trapeze with Richie Goaona, one of the world's top flyers and trainers. This is often a three-hour drive each way. Sometimes I do this twice a week. This might seem extreme, but when I climb up the ladder and jump off that pedestal, I am totally in the moment with no thoughts of my business, responsibilities, or personal challenges. It is a complete mental release. The irony is that flying on the trapeze makes me feel completely grounded like nothing else. When I am done, I hop in my car with a wide, relaxed smile on my face and drive back home to San Diego.

As of last September, I fulfilled a dream I've had for many years. I built a trapeze rig right in my own backyard – just like the ones in the circus. To be able to walk right out my back door and climb that 35-foot ladder and then fly is a magnificent feeling that I cannot even put into words. I'm sharing all of this with you to emphasize the importance of Play Days in your life. No matter what your recreational activity might be – golf, running, painting, music, or meditation – do it! Play Days will reboot your body and mind, and you will fly in your business and in your personal life like never before.

Working *on* the Business, Not *in* It

One of the first things I do with my clients is to wean them off the seven-day workweek. (Yes, most business owners work seven days a week.) I recommend that their schedules should include one weekday off, plus the entire weekend free. That leaves four full days left of work. These business owners look at me like I'm absolutely nuts. But then they try it – and guess what happens? They end up *getting more* out of the four work days than they did in seven because they are refreshed and focused. They truly value those days and their time off – whether they are golfing, boating, spending time with their families, traveling, or whatever. In addition, they find that their most innovative business ideas happen when they are outside the office taking it easy during *play*. The next goal we work toward is a three-day workweek. Once you build your solid team and systemize, this will happen. Then you will experience moments in the office in which everything is taken care of by your team and you won't know what to do with yourself. That is when you know you're on the right track.

Each person deserves a day away in which no problems are confronted, no solutions searched for. Each of us needs to withdraw from the cares which will not withdraw from us.

—*Maya Angelou, poet*

In the early entrepreneurial days, you will tend to require more Prep Days to develop your revenue streams, marketing, bookkeeping, and so on. However, as you take the leap to building your enterprise, you will want to delegate most of those tasks to your team so you can step more into the role of CEO, rather than worker bee.

My client, Robin Richter, CEO of Wearable Imaging Promotional Products – a company that has been in existence for 25 years – and a former pro golfer, used to spend crazy hours working through her elaborate order processes with her clients. Now that she has scaled with a team behind her, most of her Prep Days have shifted to Pinnacle Days. She can spend this valuable time building profitable and rewarding relationships on the golf course instead of buried behind her computer. This change was good for her bottom line and for her soul!

Most of your days during your four-day workweek will be Pinnacle Days. This is where magic can happen with your team, your partners, your clients, and your customers. This is where you are unveiling everything that was inspired during your Play Days, and then developed and honed during your Prep Days. During Pinnacle Days, you are making yourself available to everyone, listening to them, being in the moment, and soaking it all in. If you can't pare these action items down, then you need to ask yourself if you are too involved in day-to-day processes and should be delegating more.

How to Execute Your Roadmap

Now that you have your Big Picture Vision spelled out and your week divided among Prep Days, Pinnacle Days, and Play Days, you need to break down your projects and tasks into smaller steps on each day so they are actionable and achievable. A Big Picture Vision can feel exciting while at the same time seeming lofty and potentially unachievable. By working backwards and creating bite-size steps to follow on a daily basis, you will reduce the feeling of being overwhelmed, plus you will meet deadlines and achieve the goals you are working toward.

Your Mile Steps and Mini Feats

Step 1: Write out all the large steps that must happen to make your Big Picture Vision come true. This could be 10 steps or 50 steps, depending on how big your vision is. These large steps are your *Mile Steps*, your bigger projects that need to be completed in order to reach your Big Picture Vision. This could be building a website, buying a building, hiring a marketing team, or creating a new revenue stream. A Mile Step is a project that has many moving parts. It is a crucial component of making your Big Picture Vision a reality.

Step 2: Once you have this list of Mile Steps listed out, write down every step needed to complete that one project. I call these small steps your *Mini Feats*, which are minimally 20-minute incremental tasks that will help you overcome procrastination and being overwhelmed, so that you can easily move forward to completion and success.

One Mile Step may take a month or even a year to complete, depending on how large the project is and how many Mini Feats are needed to complete that project. For instance, if you are creating a franchise, adding on new locations, developing a new product, or systemizing your company, there will be many Mini Feats needed to complete that one Mile Step. For example, when building a website, your Mini Feats would be: writing copy, choosing photos, gathering testimonials, creating an opt-in, and so on.

Some of your Mini Feats will need to be repeated over and over again because you won't do them all in one sitting. By using this structure to simplify your goals in the Mile Step/Mini Feat process, you will gain a feeling of stability and reliability. When you sway off course (which can happen from time to time), simply return to your daily Mile Step/Mini Feat structure and your plans will begin moving you along your path again.

Step 3: When you are planning out your Mini Feats, schedule them on your calendar. By giving them a set time, you are much more likely to stick to them and won't try to push them off to a later time. You can also do this at www.InteractiveBusinessCoach.com

Step 4: Once you complete all of your Mile Steps, you will have reached your Big Picture Vision. Then it will be time to develop the next level of your vision.

Systemetize Everything

A longtime colleague of mine, Geeta Sidhu Robb, once said to me: "Build a business through your systems, not your blood."

Business owners like you know exactly what this means: You've put years of blood, sweat, and tears into your business. You continue to devote everything you have – time, freedom, and money – to ensure that things get done exactly the way that you want them done. Your blood might have been crucial to getting things started and, even now, you still feel like you donate 10 pints of blood each and every week. However, to stop bleeding you must move outside of yourself and get out of your own way.

Having the right systems in place right now will ultimately set you free. Your goal is to find that happy place where you have a solid and growing business that doesn't need your blood anymore, because the workflow is pumping just fine on its own. You can walk away guilt-free to focus on more important things while your team oversees the execution. But it will only work if everything is properly systematized.

As you scale your business, think carefully about all of your systems and processes. Are they as streamlined and efficient as they should be? Are you unnecessarily involved in any of the stages of execution, including approvals? What would happen if you suddenly removed yourself from the workflow – would the business collapse? Is the team capable of flying without you?

Your goal should always be to peel yourself away from executing the details and work toward creating a self-managed company. That's where your team comes in: Delegate and trust them to do their jobs!

In order to take action on tasks that lead to growth, you need powerful systems in place that accomplish the following:

1. Free you up to work on your Big Picture Vision strategy.
2. Enable your team to get from point A to point B in the most efficient manner possible without sacrificing quality.
3. Allow for new team members to step in and get into the rhythm faster with less on-boarding time.
4. Limit the number of mistakes, redos, and general churn.
5. Save your company money – unless the expenses lead to faster scaling and/or greater financial reward.
6. Rely upon as few touchpoints – i.e., checks and reviews – as possible (again, without sacrificing quality).
7. Make more money by selling and providing more products or services faster.
8. Get a higher valuation on your company when it's time to sell.

Create a Systems-Driven Culture

Upgrading your technology and recruiting the right amount of people add up to only half the equation to keep your business running at maximum efficiency. You now need to examine and fix *how* things are getting done at every stage in your workflow to be sure that tasks are:

1. Getting done properly, without anything slipping through the cracks.
2. Being completed in the most streamlined manner possible.
3. Progressing without wasted efforts or unnecessary duplication.
4. Not requiring too much oversight and/or unnecessary approvals.
5. Not cumbersome or unwieldy for your employees or you.

Become Scaleable and Salesable

By creating efficient systems and processes, you will ensure that all the right steps are being completed, that your team is working together toward a common goal, and that they are holding one another accountable. They guide your team on where to be, what to do, how to do it, and when it needs to be done. Strong processes are what will make your business *scaleable and ultimately saleable*. If you plan to sell your company one day, you need to be able to have another team step in without missing a beat. If the inner workings of your company are organized, its value will increase dramatically. Regardless of whether you plan to sell your company, take the time to set it up as if you were going to sell.

The good news is you don't need to hire Six Sigma or Kaizen experts to identify improvements in your company. Sit down with your team (freelance or in-house) leaders for quarterly planning days in which you outline existing processes, identify problems and roadblocks within those processes, and then make the pivotal decisions about which steps can be improved, replaced, shortened, or removed entirely. (This can be done virtually as well, but nothing beats face-to-face.)

Nine out of 10 times, the leader is the holdup in terms of asking for redos and dragging her feet on approvals that others can be trained and empowered to make. Be prepared to let go of a lot of control! If you demonstrate your ability to accept change, others will be willing to follow your lead.

The Systemizer

Once you have worked with your team to create a new and improved system, you don't want to lose the threads of everything that has been learned and accomplished or you'll end up reverting backwards and wasting time. This is where Systemizer comes in. This system helps direct, structure, organize, store, edit, and simplify all of the actions of your daily business. The Systemizer is the glue that holds everything together. Here are five steps to systemize your company.

> **Step 1:** Create systems for every division and operation of your company. Here is an example:
> 1.0 Onboarding
> 2.0 Administrative
> 3.0 Sales Process
> 4.0 Marketing
> 5.0 Financial
> 6.0 Legal
> 7.0 Client Trainings
> 8.0 HR/Team
> 9.0 Operations
> 10.0 Events

Step 2: Pick one of these areas and break it down into three to five subcategories and then break those subcategories down even further. This is how you determine every ongoing process, or Standard Operation Procedure (SOP), needed in your business that you can create a system around.

4.0 Marketing

    4.1 Marketing Funnels

        a. Webinars

        b. Facebook Ads

        c. Referral Program

    4.2 Social Media Posts

    4.3 Event Posts

    4.4 *Allie & You Show*

    4.5 Metrics

Step 3: Make a folder for each category. Drop in all of the tools, photos, files, and processes you already have so that you keep everything in one place. Only save items in this folder that you will continue to use. Archive old materials that you do not plan to use again.

Step 4: For each project or company process, write each step that needs to happen from start to finish and file that in your online folder.

Step 5: Create a document that lists each system, folder and the titles you have given them, so that you and your team can easily access them.

Step 6: You may also want to make a big hard-copy binder in case there is ever a technology breakdown. (Of course, that never happens, right?) Make sure to keep it updated.

SOPs serve as your mini how-to manuals on how tasks should get done in your organization. Determine which are truly the most important activities in your company that keep the wheels turning. Systemize these first and write them out in plain English as simple step-by-step instructions. One to two pages should be long enough; any longer than that and people will lose patience and refuse to use them.

Only create one or two systems per quarter because everyone needs to get in the habit of using them and it takes at least 60 days to create a new habit. You might have developed the most incredible new system but, if no one is using it, it is a complete and utter waste of time and money.

One Caveat: Don't *Over*systemetize

As much as I am screaming from the rooftops about systemizing, let me say that *over*systemetizing will have the opposite effect of what you are going for. If you have too many SOPs, they can have the reverse impact of slowing people down, confusing them, and overwhelming them. If your employees must check off, document, and report every single breath they take, they may not miss a beat – but it will take them ages to complete the task, which translates to lost time and money. Watch out for employees who realize they have a knack for churning out system and process improvements and go a little bit overboard, especially if they have been rewarded for them.

Creative left-brained people, in particular, can get bogged down with examining the minutiae of systems and processes, no matter how efficient and beneficial these processes might be. If the new way of doing things is draining creative energy from your talent, then the SOP needs, well, a new (and greatly reduced) SOP!

Let me repeat: While new systems and processes can revolutionize your company, they should always simplify – not overcomplicate.

The game has its ups and downs, but you can never lose focus of your individual goals and you can't let yourself be beat because of lack of effort.

—*Michael Jordan, NBA Hall of Famer and principal owner and chairman of the Charlotte Hornets NBA team*

GTP: Get to the Point

This is time management in a nutshell: You do the simple stuff at the beginning of the day and push the most challenging tasks toward the end of the day. When the end of the day comes, you feel frustrated that those big leaps did not happen and then you carry them to the next day.

This is just human nature. You procrastinate on the tough stuff, imagining that you can do it better later and make it flawless. In reality, this is an excuse that people hide behind. It's a way to avoid our fears and, ultimately, our dreams. Be willing to act boldly and go after the big challenges first, starting right now. Stop overthinking it. Once you make a decision, take action that moment. Write the letter, make the call, send the email – show up in a bigger way than you ever have before. But do not wait for the planets to align. Take action now and, by next week, your anxiety will start to dissipate because you are going for it. I am always so impressed by persistent people, whether they are getting the results they want or not. No matter what, if they keep pushing forward the big break they are waiting for is just one step away. Why would you ever want to miss that opportunity?

Procrastination and perfectionism can kill your company!

Get to the Point (GTP). This can apply to many things in business, but first and foremost it means taking a hard look at your To Do List and placing your Mile Steps in order based on *which ones will move your business forward the fastest.* What are the activities that will create the biggest impact on your bottom line? Some tasks might seem easy to accomplish and strike off the list – which does feel good – but they might not do a single thing to help grow your business. Other things that are complex or challenging may or may not accelerate your business, but either way, prioritize them based on the impact they have on scaling.

GTP means identifying your time wasters. Are you doing things out of obligation, fear, or guilt? Or because you are trying to show your team how hard you are working? Here's an obvious tip: Trash or reassign those activities immediately!

Here's a tough one to help you GTP and focus on the things that really matter. Ask yourself this: Does your phone really need to be on 24/7? More often than not, emails that come in are junk – or at least they can wait for a response. Having the phone on and buzzing with every single email or text can be a major distraction throughout your day. It will drive you insane. You will be amazed how much you accomplish by turning off your phone for a few hours of the day while you are concentrating on completing projects, performing revenue-generating activities, or perhaps something rewarding in the personal sense, such as hanging out with friends.

Recently, my husband (Mike) and I went to Cabo San Lucas. On arrival I turned off my phone and threw it in the drawer. I have to say, it was the most relaxing and freeing vacation I have had in a long time. I read an entire novel that was not about business and my husband and I traveled all over that island without any digital distractions! When we went to dinner, I was not anxious to jump on my phone while he went to the men's room. I was present, looking around and taking it all in. Mike and I even wrote out our entire Bucket List while we were out to dinner for my birthday.

I knew that my team had things handled. They wanted to prove to me that I did not need to check in – and I didn't. Neither do you.

Here is a challenge for you: When you are away from the office, try leaving your phone at home. Once you've begun developing your dream team, give them baby-step opportunities to be independent and run things without you … and then watch them shine. People like to step up to the plate. It gives them a sense of purpose and value.

Establishing Entrepreneurs Within Your Entrepreneurial Organization

As you run your business, you want to be 100% certain you have clearly identified the people responsible for holding other team members accountable and for overseeing proper execution of tasks. The worst thing to happen in an organization is for something to slip between the cracks and then have everyone say, "That's not my area." All of a sudden no one knows how it happened.

I once heard someone say, "If you have to tell people what to do, then you have the wrong people." There is a great deal of truth to this statement. You want a team of people who are masters of execution and get their jobs done well without churn, hesitation, and emotional wrangling. When people make inevitable mistakes, you expect them to own up to them, fix them, learn from them, and not repeat them. That is how an employee garners respect from you and her teammates. I know my team is dedicated and they work hard. They are passionate about our vision. Do they make mistakes? Yes. However, if they own them and learn from them so they are not continually repeated, they earn my respect even more.

Your role in these instances is to coach and mentor, not to dress people down or berate them for errors. If you treat people badly after giving them the opportunity to take ownership of a project, they will never admit to their mistakes again. Other employees who witness this will react the same way and constantly hide things and duck for cover.

Part of your role as leader of your business is to ensure that you have a team of people who *take responsibility for their own execution and are held accountable for all of the tasks they man-age.* I always refer to my employees as *team members.* We are all working together toward the greater good of our Big Picture Vision. When people feel like they are an important part of your vision – that their role impacts the company in a big way – they are more likely to have buy-in and do their best because they care. This is the difference between someone who sees her position as a nine-to-five job, bolting out the door before 5:01 p.m., versus someone who gives her all, until the project is done. When this happens, we all win and celebrate together as a team. If your employees are constantly making mistakes or are unmotivated, they do not see themselves as part of your team. To them, this is not a career, it is a job.

My advice: Sit down with them and ask what motivates them. What kind of growth do they see for themselves? What do they want to achieve in their life and career? What is their *why?* Then, really listen so that they feel important and seen. Share your *why*, and remind them about the company's Big Picture Vision. Help them to see they are big part of this vision, that they are here for a reason, and that you cannot do it without them. Then, ask them: "Now that you know how important your role is, how do you feel you can best contribute to this vision? How does it support your own vision?"

Unless that person is not a good fit or doesn't have the potential to step into the skill set you need, she will rise to the occasion. Everyone wants to feel purposeful and appreciated. If you can accomplish this with your team, you will witness their energy and passion soar like a circus artist performing a double back flip on the trapeze or an Olympic snowboarder performing daring tricks in a half-pipe competition.

> If you want to build a ship, don't drum up people to collect wood and don't assign them tasks and work, but rather teach them to long for the endless immensity of the sea.
> —*Antoine de Saint-Exupéry, writer, poet, and pioneering aviator*

Inspect What You Expect

I bet I know what you are going to say next: "I delegated *A*, *B*, and *C* to three different members of my team. *A* veered off in the completely wrong direction. *B* never got the job done. *C* screwed things up. How can I possibly empower people and trust them with important tasks when I know they won't get them done right, if they get done at all?"

Ask yourself: "Did your employees receive enough training?", "Were expectations made clear to them?" and "Did you have checkpoints along the way to ensure they were on track?"

Your team members are human beings and will make mistakes, just like you did (and still do). They don't own the business, so they won't do things exactly the way you would. They are not going to eat, sleep, and breathe your company the way you do. By the same token, if they don't improve with all the training provided, then you need to make that difficult call. Remember, what got you here will not necessarily get you to the next level. You need to decide if the team you have will go the extra mile. These are often difficult decisions, so trust your gut; if you know the right answer, don't wait to follow through. Time slips quickly through your fingers and, before you know it, another year goes by, and then another. When you finally make that much-needed decision, you ask yourself: "Why did I not make the move when I first had an inkling?" As you take that leap from entrepreneur to enterprise, take the team with you that is ready to fly high!

There's no half-singing in the shower. You're either a rock star or an opera diva.
—*Josh Groban, singer, songwriter, and record producer*

In my company, there are so many moving parts in all of our launches and product releases and events that sporadic "inspections" prove to be invaluable for everyone concerned. This type of quality control also demonstrates the important advantage of having an in-house staff rather than freelancers. It's difficult to have regular inspections with freelancers because they work at their own pace and on their own schedules. It's also difficult communicating SOPs – some of which may even be confidential – when you are working with independent contractors, even if you have signed confidentiality agreements.

I admit that execution may not be the most glamorous or exciting part of the scaling process. Even so, keep in mind that when an audience is watching athletic teams in action, all they see is the end result of everything: *the execution*. If your team follows well-thought-out systems and processes and acts like entrepreneurs, your products and services will achieve everything you envisioned and more. Your customers will applaud you and your team with rave reviews, repeat business, and glowing recommendations and referrals – all of which will lead to scaling and creating your dream enterprise.

Chapter Summary: You've Got This!

- DO create systems and processes that help you accomplish your Big Picture Vision.
- DO systematize your company with the Three Ps.
- DON'T allow your company to *over*systematize.
- DO make sure you GTP (Get to the Point) in all aspects of business execution and communication.
- DO create a culture of entrepreneurs who can independently execute tasks.
- DO allow room for checkpoints along the way for major projects and investments.

7

The Healthy and Wealthy CEO

All that we are is the result of what we have thought.

—Buddha

Not All Car Crashes Are Bad

In the early stages of my business career, I studied homeopathy with the goal of opening up my own private practice. After my experience running myself over with my car (as described in Chapter 1), homeopathy had a profound impact on my healing. The more I learned about it, the more passionate I became about this gentle, yet powerful form of medicine.

At the time, I was a single mom living month to month and had a deep commitment to create a passionate and successful life for my daughter and myself. I was also doing my best to surround myself with positive people who believed in making their impossible dreams reality.

As I neared the end of my homeopathic education, I found myself $6,000 short of paying the balance of my tuition. I went to my mom to ask her for support. She answered, "No, you need to get a job."

My mom's harsh answer was coming from a place of fear. She was concerned that I had gone off the deep end by walking away from a successful ad agency, which was killing me and ending my marriage. She even asked me if homeopathy was a religious cult!

I had always viewed my mom as my biggest fan. However, like many naysayers, she was projecting her own fears onto me. Her worry translated to negativity. My craving for a passionate life, along with my ingrained stubbornness, kept me hopeful and positive in my bleakest moments. I refused to forget that it could be much worse. I could still be lonely in my marriage. I could still be burned out and miserable, the way I was in my early business. I learned to put my head down, move intently forward in my beliefs, and refuse to listen to anyone who was negative or unsupportive. The more they said, "You can't," the more determined I became.

The same day I spoke to my mother, I drove up the beach in Del Mar where I often went to think through my challenges.

While I was parked, I closed my eyes and meditated on a solution. Suddenly, the rear of my car was jolted from behind by another car.

Normally one would consider this a bad thing. But I was relatively uninjured and ended up receiving a check from the insurance company for – drum roll, please – $6,000! Talk about miraculous coincidences!

I had refused to back down on my dreams and, since then, my wealth has multiplied into many millions. My mom now always says to me, "Thank goodness you didn't listen!"

I learned from this experience that, if you are 100% clear in your mind about what you truly desire, and if you fully believe you will attain it, ultimately you will attract what you want. It may not happen in exactly the way you imagined it, but that is the beauty of life. Things may not happen precisely according to plan but, if you are open to miracles while on your journey, your vision will fall into place and can be even better than you hoped it would.

You, too, can scale your dream business. Conjure it, flesh it out, nurture it, get ongoing mentoring and direction – and then have faith that everything will eventually come together at the right time and place.

■ ■ ■

When I think of the phrase "the human race," I visualize millions of people bursting from the starting gate and running through life with only one purpose: "Get to the finish line!" A race is defined as a contest between two or more people seeking to do or reach the same thing first. What's missing from this definition is that it does not embody the idea of getting in touch with the process of all the "in-between stuff" – the single moments that make up each day on Earth.

When you are in the process of scaling your business, you need to stop thinking about being in any kind of a race. Yes, you are moving toward your desired destination. You are attracting your Big Picture Vision with every decision that you make.

I challenge you to stop throughout the day, take big deep breaths, and open your eyes fully. Stopping to smell the roses may seem trite. However, I practice this daily and it has given so many more moments of pure bliss and joy. Exercise living in the moment and being happy in the "now" as you are heading toward your Big Picture Vision. As a driven, type A CEO, you are most likely focused solely on your goals, which is important. However, if you are so singularly focused that you miss out on the star-studded landscape around you and the little miracles falling at your feet on a daily basis, you will arrive at your destination with years of missed opportunities for happiness.

As the leader of your organization, you need to be mentally, physically, emotionally, and spiritually healthy in order to achieve your Big Picture Vision. This chapter will help you become well rounded and happier through all the ups and downs as your business expands, instead of being constantly stressed out while chasing your tail. You deserve all the success and happiness you create – so enjoy it!

From the Rat Race to the Human Journey

As you continue to expand your business, the stakes will seem to rise and the complications and complexities will multiply. Nothing will get easier for you on the outside, however, you have the opportunity to work on yourself to become more resilient so that whatever is collapsing around you rolls off your back. It's easy to get caught up in the mania of the rat race in which work leads you, instead of you leading it. The energy of our lives moves forward at an alarming rate. Just look in the rearview mirror while you're driving on the freeway. Everyone is heading forward in high gear to *get somewhere else*. Most of the drivers are more focused on what's happening next, rather than being present in the journey. This is the "Living-Outside-of-the-Body Syndrome" – a state of complete disconnection with the present moment.

The fact is, business will be stressful for you – if that is how you perceive it. The unexpected happens every day. Things go wrong all the time: equipment breaks down, customers get lost, employees (and you) make mistakes, proposals get rejected. You can't control many of these things, but you can control how you react (or overreact) to them. How you handle your stress levels will determine your scaling success and overall happiness.

Mark my words: The more you attempt to live life to the fullest, the more you will expose yourself to diversified tones of energy and experiences. Well, *thank goodness for those surprises!* 'Cause let's be honest. You would be bored to tears if life were controlled and predictable. You may crave complete calmness but, if you had it all the time, you would be looking for another opportunity with more excitement. You are a maverick business owner, after all. And this is the pace of our times.

So, how can we manage the "racy ride" in a calmer and more fulfilling way? Is it even possible to live a full life while taking the stressful times in stride? Can you prevent burnout? Can you get everything done without losing your soul and spirit in the process?

Yes, you can!

There are many ways to slow down the pace without sacrificing your intent. Remember, productivity could be a waste of your precious time if your intention is to just get things done and off your list. I've had many people tell me that they cannot sit and relax until "everything is done."

Think about this. When is "everything at work" (or anywhere) ever completely "done"? *Never.* If that were the case you would be retired or under the ground. So business owners spend their lives trying to accomplish their endless task list, hoping that someday they can stop and enjoy their lives. They are so driven and so focused on "the goal" that, even when they reach it, they're already off to the next one. They're not taking it in, celebrating their accomplishment, and experiencing what they have drawn into their lives.

Sure, we all want to make more money. But hitting that money jackpot while being miserable in the process is definitely not worth its weight in gold. I am not saying that working hard is always going to be rainbows and bunny rabbits, but even the tough days can be beautiful if you are fueled by your underlying *why* and a deeper sense of purpose.

> If your only goal is to become rich, you will never achieve it.
> —*John D. Rockefeller, business magnate, industrialist, and philanthropist*

The crux of it is this: If you are stuck in the rat race and are only going after the biggest piece of cheese, you might become a millionaire or even a billionaire. Yet you will never become a *happy* millionaire or billionaire because you were focused only on the end goal – not the thrilling human journey along the way. Most highly successful business owners are driven by a deeper purpose well beyond money. Believe me, I feel that money is a great thing! The more I earn, the more people I can help elevate and the more causes I can get behind. However, if money were my only goal, I would have quit long ago, never staying the course through the tough days.

Your Personal Energy Bank

One way to reclaim your true self in business and in life is to find out where the energy leaks reside, so that you can begin to repair them. Then you can focus your energy in a direction that is feeding you – not draining you.

Everything is made of energy. This is the law of quantum physics. If you look at a table or a couch under an electron microscope, you'll see that they are actually made up of atoms in constant motion – just like your body. All of these things are constantly changing and never standing still.

Similarly, you have the ability to create and change your reality in every moment. How powerful is that? Your thoughts and actions also operate from this precious field of energy. Your thoughts are powerful. Even simple actions start with a basic but mighty thought. You think to take a step – and then you take a step. When you think to raise your arm, your arm elevates. Since thoughts are energy, it makes sense to choose positive thoughts and actions that benefit you by replenishing and expanding your supply of energy – not draining it.

Instead of stressing about all of the things that you can't control and will deplete your energy bank, why not rechannel that energy into your Big Picture Vision? Visualize unplugging from negativity around you or a circumstance that is getting you down and then plugging into something that makes you happy. Focus on potential solutions or the lessons learned for a better next outcome. Or, better yet, why not go to bed at night with some reserve energy for the next day?

Letting Go of Some of Your To Do's

Success is about figuring out what you want your business life to look like. How do you want to spend your time at work? If you're doing everything yourself and micromanaging your team, you are depleting your energy bank and you probably won't achieve your scaling goals or your Big Picture Vision.

In Chapter 6, I emphasized the importance of taking time for Play Days in your weekly schedule. In Chapter 5, I covered various ways to becoming a great leader: decision-making, delegating, staying focused, listening, treating your team as equals, and so on.

Here, in this chapter, let's consider the toll that wearing too many hats in your company is taking on your health. When was the last time you had a physical checkup? Are you eating right? Do you exercise? And here's the biggie: Are you stressed out all the time?

Many entrepreneurs are horrible at self-care because they are so focused on taking care of everyone and everything besides themselves. They rush through lunch, eating junk that is not bolstering their bodies or minds. They might think about exercising, but instead they choose to deal with the pile of papers on the desk or prioritize putting out a fire over heading to the gym. It's always about "getting one more thing done." Before they know it, the day is over and they have no time or energy to work out. Can you relate?

I don't mean to get on your case, but here's the thing: You can't afford *not* to exercise. Your stress levels will get out of control, your muscles will tense up and atrophy, and your heart will become congested mush. What good are you to your team, your family, and your business if you end up in a hospital bed?

On the other hand, an hour of exercise a day loosens those muscles, gets the blood pumping, releases endorphins throughout your body ... and guess what? You feel like you have accomplished something, your mood has improved, and you have a positive outlook on life. After a good workout you feel as though you can accomplish anything. Exercise is a *must* on your daily To Do list.

As you scale your business, be aware that *you're the one who is trying to replace yourself.* You need to practice honing your courage to let go and find people who can handle some of your To Do's. This will enable you to make a priority of exercising, eating right, and getting enough sleep, so you can experience the ultimate freedom: good health. The goal is to free yourself from the day-to-day, be able to step away for a month or two instead of a day or two, and have your business continue to grow with the team and systems you now have in place. If you're overworked and stressed out, it's because you're working *in* the business and not *on* the business – and that must change.

Just Say "No"

I have become much better at saying "no." This has taken much practice over the years by peeling away the people-pleasing tendencies that I've had since childhood. The bigger you company grows, the more "no's" you will need to express. Setting boundaries for yourself must become a regular part of your daily practice. This could mean saying "no" to the big things – a business deal or opportunity that may seem exciting, but won't move you toward your Big Picture Vision – or the smaller things, such as choosing the color of a sales page or signing off on an outgoing email. It really is okay to say "no." And, as hard as it might feel to say "no" or hand it off, the immediate relief afterwards and instant boost in self-confidence is worth every moment of standing up for yourself.

In fact, I would go as far as stating that "*no* is the new *yes*." The more you say "no" and set boundaries for yourself and your organization, the more time you'll have to devote to the things that really matter. If you are living your life based on other people's terms by saying "yes" to everything, you end up becoming dependent on those terms. All of those individuals, in turn, become reliant on you. That sounds wonderful on the surface, doesn't it? It feels good to be needed and that people celebrate you when you say "yes."

Life Is an Energy Mirror

Your surroundings are merely a mirror of your inner beliefs.

Your reality is a mirror of your internal thoughts and feelings. For example, a person who is convinced that most new businesses fail shouldn't start one. Why? Because this thought becomes a self-fulfilling prophecy and it probably will fail.

Internal energy can be extremely powerful. I know that some of you are thinking, "I don't express those negative thoughts;

I just think them." I have news for you: Even if you're not voicing your fears or beliefs, you are emitting a negative frequency into the atmosphere with your negative thought.

Now this doesn't mean that every single negative thought will create more negativity or lost opportunities in your life. However, if you continue to focus on your limiting beliefs, your life will begin to reflect that same internal energy. As bestselling author and motivational speaker Wayne Dyer said, "If you change the way you look at things, the things you look at change."

The good news is that this is reversible. Once internal negative thoughts are replaced with winning beliefs, your external world will begin to change in a dramatic way.

As you've gathered by now, homeopathy has been a big part of my life. I ran my homeopathic practice for almost 20 years and worked with thousands of patients, families, and children. From my experiences I discovered that what tends to make people sick and out of balance is when they are not living congruently. In layperson's terms, the concept of homeopathy is that the body cannot hold two like diseases – one cancels out the other. So it is all about matching the energy of the substance to the energy of the body.

If you tend to focus on being afraid of things going wrong, guess what? They will go wrong. Your mirror is projecting your fears back at you and causing the result you convinced yourself would happen.

However, if you stay connected to your Big Picture Vision – even when you feel some fear – you can refocus your mindset and flip around the mirror. Feeling a certain amount of fear is normal, but when it turns into the "fight or flight" primitive response – such as reacting as if you are being chased by a dangerous animal and your instincts compel you to run, but in truth it is a harmless little dog – it's going way too far. You will make emotional and unwise choices that keep you small, and your health will be impacted from the flood of stress-inducing adrenaline. As one of my mentors once said to me, "When you face a challenge that you have confronted in the past, try reacting differently." It seems simple, but in reality it takes focused effort to work against old habits. New actions create new results. Get support, be willing to fail, do what you need to do to face the fear, and move through it. All the magic is waiting for you on the other side of your fear.

Deaccentuate the Negative

The energy mirror is all around you in your business life, whether you realize it or not. This means exactly what you think: If you surround yourself with positive people, positive things will happen. If you surround yourself with toxic people, well ... you get the picture.

In my company, I don't hire negative people and I don't retain positive people who turn negative, since their attitudes begin to impact their colleagues and sometimes even me. I refuse to work with negative clients. I strive for a positive environment at all times and you should expect the same in your company.

Of course, everyone has a bad day. A lapse every now and then is understandable. We are human, after all. It goes without saying that everyday disagreements, honest opinions, and reality checks don't necessarily make a person negative. Differing perspectives and points of view are welcome in an organization, even if they don't mesh with yours all of the time.

Then you have the Debbie Downers of the world – the people who believe everything will fail, fall apart, and come crashing down. You know these individuals: They are solely focused on the problem, not the solution. They become so wrapped up in the negative outcomes that they don't realize that *they are the problem.*

The Happiest Person I Know

Dr. Sean Stephenson is an amazing therapist, author, and motivational speaker. He is enormously successful and has been speaking in front of audiences since he was 17 years old. His message has reached over 300,000,000 people worldwide. I had the honor of having Sean speak at one of my recent events.

Here's the capper: Sean is three feet tall and suffers from a genetic disorder, *Osteogenesis Imperfecta*, often referred to as brittle bone disease. He has experienced more pain than anyone should ever have to.

Did Sean give in to negativity? Not a chance. He graduated with a doctorate degree, changed his eating habits, developed his own exercise program, married a brilliant and beautiful woman, and put his disability in the rear-view mirror. He worked for US President Bill Clinton in the White House, surrounds himself with other amazing self-improvement and business minds, has an international best-selling book (published in a dozen languages), and now spends his time counseling entrepreneurs and running his own speaker-training seminars.

Most all, Sean is the happiest person I know. He is unbelievably confident. As a little boy, when his bones were breaking, his mom would ask him: "Are you going to make this a burden or a blessing?" You know which path Sean chose. He says his mission is to rid the world of insecurity.

As a result of his positive energy and unrelenting determination, Sean has created a sensational life for himself. If he can do it, what's stopping you? Really, what do you have to complain about?

Negative energy is highly contagious. Suppose you were up on the trapeze and about to leap in the air when your catcher shouts, "I can't do it ... I'm going to miss! It didn't work last time, it won't work this time!"

Would you feel comfortable taking that leap? No way! That negativity would flood your mind causing a panic attack and you would remain frozen on that platform.

The same goes in business. You want people on your team whom you trust and are right there with you every step of the way.

Get Out of the Fight and into the Flow

Dismissing negative thoughts is easier said than done, right? The more you try to tune them out and heal yourself, the more they seem to fill your head. So, what are you supposed to do?

Earlier in this chapter I mentioned the importance of going to the gym and exercising. But sometimes that's not enough – and there are times late at night when exercise is not realistic, but the problems are festering and keeping you awake.

Part of being healthy and healing yourself is being able to do things that do not involve financial gain. I know – that's a really hard thing for a business owner like you to do. However, if you don't disconnect from business, eventually negative thoughts will catch up with you and suffocate you. In the pages that follow are some techniques to help you relax, clear your head, and get back in the flow.

Write It to Release It

Journaling can be an excellent way to rid yourself of negative thoughts. You don't have to be a brilliant author – or even a writer at all – to get started. All you need is a good notebook and your pen of choice.

First, find yourself a quiet, comfortable spot. Don't think – just starting scribbling down whatever is on your mind. Let the words flow. By writing in a stream of consciousness style, you release the emotions attached to the things that are troubling you. The process becomes cathartic, even if solutions to the problems don't immediately present themselves. It also happens that, if you are writing in the middle of the night, you will find it relaxing and eventually will become tired enough to drift off to sleep.

I had a situation years ago that was really troubling me. I felt resentful to a now ex-business partner who had done something dishonest behind my back. Even though I confronted her with the issue, I was continuing to have nightmares about it. In the dream I was yelling at her about how I really felt. I awoke completely shaken up. I finally decided to journal about it in the middle of the night. I allowed myself to express every angry word and emotion that I was feeling right onto the page. Wouldn't you know it, the angry dreams stopped. I let it go and moved on.

Passion Feeds Your Soul

On second thought, maybe you *are* a writer and writing is your passion. Or, maybe it's something else: art, photography, singing, painting, sculpture, building or repairing things, knitting, scrapbooking, or something else that floats your boat. Or, maybe it's a sport: tennis, bowling, skiing, biking, climbing, and so on. Whatever your hobby or interest might be, make time for it!

It's crucial for you, as a business owner, to be involved in a passionate activity outside your company, otherwise you run the risk of becoming a single-focused, compulsive, workaholic individual. Been there, done that – and I don't recommend it. When you are engrossed in a non-work-related passion project, the sting of the problems troubling you will fade out. This is when you will do your most revolutionary, innovative thinking and will come up with solutions to many of your dilemmas. It's also one of the reasons I love the trapeze so much. When I am up on that pedestal and flipping through the air, you better believe I am 100% in the moment. And, for that nanosecond, all of life's challenges melt away. This is my moving meditation. I feel like I am just getting started and plan to be the first centenarian flyer around. If you would like to see me fly, go to: www.ScaleorFail .com/trapeze.

Jin Shin Acutouch Treatment: A Step-by-Step Self-Treatment

Here's a treatment that you can give to yourself for immediate stress relief while sitting in your car or lying in bed at night. I use it all the time when I can't sleep, feel any physical pain, or just need to find calm in a stressful moment. It may seem a little odd – but believe me, it works!

1. Put your right hand on top of your head, palm down. Hold it there firmly until Step 6.
2. Put your left hand on your forehead. Hold it there for one minute.
3. Place two fingers from your left hand under your nose so that the bottom finger rests at the top of your upper lip. Hold your fingers there for one minute.
4. Put your left hand on your chest for one minute.
5. Put your left hand on your diaphragm for one minute.
6. Position your left hand so that it covers your belly button and hold it there for one minute.
7. Position your left hand so that it is on your pubic bone and continue to hold it there as you move your right hand under your tailbone.
8. Hold these last points for one minute.

You may already feel calmer by the time you get halfway through the exercise. Try it at bedtime and you may fall asleep before you finish.

Get a Coach

Let me make this perfectly clear: A coach is not the equivalent of a therapist. The two may intersect at some points – human beings aren't quite so compartmentalized – but a therapist is there mainly to help you cope with past and present mental and emotional trauma and personal issues. A business mentor, however, can objectively work with you to lay out your business strategy, help you make paramount decisions that will impact your growth, and get you to where you want to go without all the crazy twists and turns most business owners take. A good coach or mentor will consider your emotional makeup, personality quirks, and work style to help identify root causes of the things that might be holding you back from achieving your success.

I don't know you at all, so I won't speak to whether I think you need a therapist or not. But I do recommend that you and every business owner find a trusted business coach. The most successful CEOs in the world have coaches, including the presidents of Google and Intuit. Even Steve Jobs had a coach.

Finding a coach who has "been there, done that" in business will get you where you want to go in a fraction of the time. They are like the geo-force behind your dreams. It may only take one year instead of five to accomplish them, which saves you hundreds of thousands of dollars in opportunity cost. Business coaches can help stop you from spinning in circles, wasting months or even years of deliberating on things. They can help guide you to listening to your inner voice. As outlined in Chapter 6, they can also help you extricate yourself from execution details that you have no business continuing to do on a daily basis. I also like to say that business and life will intersect and there is no getting around that. When life shows up with challenges, it can't help but affect your business. Having a mentor to bounce off the life stuff helps to keep your head on straight so business can go on as usual.

Another great way to gain amazing insights and network opportunities is to join or create a "mastermind" group, as described by Napoleon Hill in *Think and Grow Rich* and later named by Jayson Gaignard in his book, *Mastermind Dinners*. A mastermind group is designed to help you navigate challenges using the collective intelligence of others.

The gist of it is this: Let's say that I invite five clients or noted experts over for a dinner party. The only caveat for the guests is that they need to invite one or two businesspeople that they know. You might say something like, "Look, I love working with you. You know we're a good fit. Who else do you know that's like you that could potentially benefit from my services?"

I have had a business coach and been in a mastermind group for many years and this relationship and strategy has proven invaluable to me. It is what has given me the pathway to make tens of millions of dollars and be the catalyst of change for so many. Even when things are cruising along and going well, there is always something new that I am learning.

Find a magnificent coach – join a mastermind group of like-minded individuals to lift you up – and build a solid support team. These individuals will help you get through the rough patches and can provide insights and expertise on everything from recruiting to marketing to leadership to systemizing your company.

These individuals are cheering you on every single day – and so am I!

Chapter Summary: You've Got This!

- DO yourself a favor and get out of the rat race.
- DO manage your energy bank.
- DON'T allow your To Do list to ruin your mental, physical, spiritual, and emotional health.
- DO learn to say "no."
- DO listen to your inner voice.
- DON'T work with negative people.
- DO try journaling and developing a hobby to create positive flow in your life.
- DO try my breathing exercise and the Jin Shin Acutouch Treatment to reduce stress.
- DO surround yourself with a powerful network of support people.

Money and Mindset

I had to make my own living and my own opportunity. But I made it. Don't sit down and wait for the opportunities to come. Get up and make them!
—Madame C. J. Walker, entrepreneur, philanthropist, and activist

My Story of Synchronicity and Faith

At the same time that I walked away from my ad agency years ago, I also chose to leave a difficult marriage. I was at a major crossroads. I was working toward launching my homeopathic practice. I had a whole new life ahead of me, a child to raise, and no money in the bank. Back then I was surrounded by people who believed my decisions and choices were all wrong, and they were vocal about it. They were unwilling to get behind me financially or emotionally. I was driving a green Ford Taurus at the time that cost me a whopping $3,000. Every day I dropped my daughter off at school something would fall off the car, such as the door handle or rearview mirror. My daughter would look at me as if to say, "Really mom, this is pathetic!" I was scared and my back was against the wall. I honestly had nowhere to go but up.

I remember one pivotal moment when I wanted to meet a friend for coffee, but didn't have enough cash to pay for myself. I went through my closet and emptied out all of my purses. I managed to cobble together a few bucks and some change and join my friend at the coffee shop. When I went to the register to place my order, I blindly reached into my purse, gathered up the change, and placed the crumped bills and loose coins on the counter. I will never forget this because it was the exact cost of the coffee to the last penny.

This was my sign. I was at my lowest point, scraping and struggling to get by. But I realized that, if I followed my heart, all that I needed would appear. I had to stay determined and follow along my path, regardless of what others believed I should or should not do. Somehow I would be taken care of.

I haven't looked back since then. Thirty years and nine businesses later, I am thriving. I am so glad I held firm and never caved in to my fear.

■ ■ ■

I chose "money and mindset" as the subject for this last chapter for one reason: Scaling a business is not for the faint of heart. It takes a willingness to experience extreme discomfort, bumpy roads, long periods of gasping financial uncertainty, and possibly creating discord with loved ones leading to the end of relationships. You might be thinking, why would anyone put herself through so much agony?

Never forget this: Living your truth and expressing what really matters to you in this world is an absolute blessing. You could play it safe, live a mediocre life, and never allow your dreams to play out. Or, you can realize you have one life – so why wouldn't you want to live it to the fullest? To be able to have the freedom of choice to take an idea and turn it into a product or service that solves someone's pain or longing requires deep dedication and sacrifice. Those who truly believe in you and understand the importance of going after your dreams will hang in there during those challenging growth times. The monetary pay off and sense of accomplishment that "you did it, despite all odds" will be worth every moment of uneasiness along the way. Your success relies on your ability to own your self-confidence, persistence, and resilience – no matter what is thrown at you on any given day.

In the beginning of our business relationship, some clients say to me: "I don't need help with my mindset. My mindset is great and I don't need to focus on that."

> Abundance is not something we acquire. It is something that we tune into.
> —*Wayne Dyer, bestselling author and motivational speaker*

My response: "Well, you must be a billionaire!"

The fact is, every time you grow to the next level you are going to have to face a whole new round of challenges. *Remember:*

In the immortal words of executive coach and bestselling author Marshall Goldsmith, "what got you here, won't get you there." As the saying goes, "new level, new devil." It can get scarier as you scale because you have more to lose – and you need to have your mindset in check every step of the way. All of your deep-seated issues – *Am I worthy?*, *Am I strong enough?*, *Am I smart enough?*, and *Am I up to the task?* – will come up front and center. So will the irrational fears of things beyond your control going wrong: *Will the economy collapse? Will our customers stop buying from me? Will our customers go out of business? Will my costs shoot through the roof? Will my competition eat my lunch?*

It is only when your back is thrown up against the wall that your true colors appear. Do you have the mental toughness to take it? Can you roll up your sleeves and do whatever is necessary is stay the course?

Each time you overcome your inherent demons, your skin thickens. If you stick with your Big Picture Vision and keep moving forward instead of retreating in fear, you will become more resilient and bounce back faster with each setback.

No matter what state your business is in at the moment – surviving, growing, or scaling – you must be aware that setbacks and disasters are inevitable. They are going to happen. *At any time.*

In order to successfully grow and scale your business when these calamities occur, you need to look yourself straight in the mirror on these occasions and say the following: "I'm stronger than this. I'm going to do something about it. My dream is too important to give up!"

When you elevate who you are and you see that you are bigger than the obstacle, worry, or stress you are facing, you don't allow it to take over your mindset. When you are feeling strong and confident, you don't allow any of those things to shake you. You separate the challenges from who you are, so you don't take them personally and can deal with them head-on.

If you hit a rough period in your company, first, don't freak out. Give yourself the frame of mind to brainstorm what solutions might exist. Then consult with other people. Come up with a plan. Come up with a back-up plan. Then come up with a backup to the backup plan. Ask yourself: How can I reposition and tap into what already has momentum? How can I leverage?

—Excerpt from my interview with Roland Frasier, principal, digital marketer, attorney, and serial entrepreneur. For the full interview, go to: www.ScaleorFaleBook.com/bonus.

Never Cash Out Early Due to Fear

When the stock market spirals downward, it's known as a *crash.* When people react to market shifts by rushing to sell off their stocks, it's known as *panic selling. Crash* and *panic selling* are not positive terms! The folks who unload their stock in a panic are reacting emotionally and ignoring all investing fundamentals. They often lose a ton of money in opportunity cost. Fear is the *worst way* to manage your stock portfolio *because it will never grow.* You are bailing out before allowing anything positive to happen. You have to take some risks and ride things out in order to meet with success.

It's no different at the poker table. Is a nervous poker player going to win the pot? Never. Every time a fearful player has a bad hand or is bluffing, he'll break out in a sweat, bite his nails, rub his chin, or show some other involuntary sign. He'll lose every single time. Meanwhile, the calm, cool cucumber wearing shades stays the course and cleans up the table.

Since we are already on the subject of gambling, here's one more analogy: Think about the slot machines. You've put quarters in the same machine all day. You've blown $100 and are ready to throw in the towel. As soon as you leave, a 90-year-old lady with a cigarette dangling from her lips and a cup of quarters plunks herself down on your chair while it's still warm. She puts a coin in, pulls the lever, and guess what – JACKPOT!

I'm sure that your company has a far better business model than playing the slot machines. And hopefully it's not quite as volatile as the stock market. In any case, do not let fear – or *any emotion*, for that matter – dictate what you do with your business. Your mindset needs to be free, clear, and focused at all times to make the right business decisions, especially when bad things happen.

The Money Mindset: It's Just Business

We've established that you need to separate your emotions from your business thinking. Let's take that a step further. You have to see your business as a *separate entity from yourself as an investment.* Your business has the capability of providing for your family, employing a team of people, paving the way for your eventual retirement, supporting generations to come, and making a long term impact on business and society. If you view your company as a *personal* asset rather than as a *separate investment entity*, you are putting all of those things at risk because you have the wrong money mindset. Consider the following scenarios:

- Hiring your son-in-law for a key executive position even though everyone thinks he is clueless.
- Passing on buying out a major competitor because your child is going to an expensive college the following year.
- Leaving key positions unfilled because you hear an economic downturn might be looming.
- Not hiring that business coach because you are remodeling your house.
- Cutting the marketing budget before the plan is launched because revenue is below expectations for the month.

- Selling your business for much less than it would be worth if you took the time to put the right systems and team in place.

Variations of the above situations occur all too frequently in private businesses. Admit it: You are guilty at one time or another of at least one of these cardinal mindset sins. Have you hired a family member for an ill-suited position because the personal decision outweighed the business decision?

The Stuck Mindset

A client of mine, Steve Miccio – CEO of Projects at Empower, a company that developed a unique process to heal people with addictions using a nonmedical approach – has this to say about the time he spent being stuck:

> We were growing over the past seven years, but I was losing sleep. I was at the end of my rope, not sure where I was going or what I was doing. I was losing my vision, which is tough when you are a visionary. I was so buried and stuck in the minutia and in the mode of fixing, instead of taking leaps to grow and scale. In my mind I was looking at building this to a $20 million company in the next five years, but through working with Allison's team, I realized I have at least a $300 million company in front of me. What I realized is that I wasn't giving myself value. I had forgotten that I had created something that is going to change the mental health system toward addictions around the world and transform millions of lives.

Steve started thinking and acting much bigger. He increased his staff from 30 to 90. In less than one year, he's signed a $4 million contract with a hospital to get people to a better place in their lives.

I have no doubt that there has been at least one occasion in which you felt like Steve when he was stuck. You were buried in your business and didn't realize that by "thinking small choices" you were keeping yourself there. For instance, there was probably a time when you needed to hire someone for an important position, but put it off for weeks or months because you were worried about cash flow or how long it would take for the money to come in. Meanwhile, you lost money from projects and opportunities that fell through the cracks due to lack of bandwidth on your team. Plus, your team became utterly confused about what was happening about that position and was buzzing over these questions:

- Will this crucial role ever be filled?
- Is the business in such poor shape we can't afford to bring someone in for a job that is so important?
- Is my job at risk?
- How long will I have to keep covering tasks that should be done by someone filling this position?
- I'm burned out and have no passion for what I do anymore.

The end result: turmoil. Your team gets into panic mode. They lose focus. They burn out. They look for other jobs. Massive turnover. And it's all because you allowed yourself to think of your business as a personal asset, not a business asset, and did not fill a critical role that would keep your engines humming and your train moving forward.

Your money mindset must always be to hire the best team players that you can possibly attract – and then work every day to retain them. If your mindset is that you are always worried about cash flow and its impact on your personal finances, your team will pick up on this and they will be unable to serve the organization to the best of their ability. If you, the leader, are overly cautious and afraid, mark my words: Your team is imagining everyone falling off the trapeze and the circus leaving town.

Having the right money mindset for scaling means never acting as if you are in survival mode – even during the most challenging times. Do not allow personal matters to influence your business thinking. When you enter the front door of your home, then you can take off your business hat and focus 100% on your family and yourself.

A Mindset of Abundance

Money is a tangible thing, but it can also be regarded as a state of mind. When you learn to visualize wealth and a life of abundance, you can channel that as energy and tap into it as needed. A positive mindset will super charge you into action that will lead to achieving your desired results. On the flip side, a negative mindset is the easiest way to wreck your financial health.

Consider this:

Thoughts = your feelings = your actions = results

If your thoughts are "What if I lose my money?," you will become anxious about money. If you are anxious about money, your actions are going to be cautious. The result of being cautious is that you won't see any financial growth.

However, if your thoughts are "There's abundance everywhere!," your feelings will be happy and your actions will be bold in creating new revenue streams. The result of this is that your business will flourish.

My husband and I have a saying when we are writing a big check: "There's more where that came from!" It's a cliché, but an important one in our mindsets. Instead of feeling as if spending is a burden and high risk, we *celebrate* it. We are paying attention to every penny that comes in and goes out and believe that, when money goes elsewhere, the business will expand.

Fears, for the most part, are memories from past experiences, things you saw on TV, something your parents, friends, or teachers said, or you read in books. They are in your memory bank as an emotion that can bring up a potential negative consequence. It is the potential consequence that is bringing up the emotion. You are projecting into the future and feeling it in the present moment. You can release these fears and other emotions through raising your level of awareness knowledge and skill instead of being a victim of fear.

—Excerpt from my interview with John Assaraf,
CEO and founder of NeuroGym. For the full interview,
go to: www.ScaleorFail.com/bonus.

Think of Yourself As a Gourmet

There's a story – perhaps apocryphal, but that's okay – about cake that has relevance here. (Yes, that's right: cake!) A supermarket set up a taste test with two tables: one for a "gourmet" cake versus another for a "regular" cake. No brands were mentioned – only whether the cake was gourmet or not. Guess which won? The gourmet cake, of course – by a landslide. When asked, tasters said they would pay *double* for the gourmet cake over the regular one. It turns out, both cakes were made from the exact same ingredients and by the same baker. They were exactly the same. But why did so many people choose the "gourmet" cake over the "regular" one?

The answer is obvious: Just the word "gourmet" alone gave a perception of it being upscale, better tasting, and having more intrinsic value. Unless you are in a low-end market by intent and this is integral to your business strategy, always think of yourself as a gourmet and consider your products luxurious.

The Myth That All Consumers Buy the Cheapest

Yes, smart shoppers will try to find coupons and discounts and look to buy their favorite products at the lowest possible prices. Amazon.com and Walmart have dominated the retail price wars and pretty much everyone else has steered clear of the battlefield.

But think about your favorite, most sinfully decadent ice cream. Or your most comfortable, stylish shoes. Or your most professional-looking handbag or briefcase. Or your fanciest power pen of choice. Would you really think to buy any of these products on Amazon.com or in a Walmart? I don't think so.

A pint of Good Humor ice cream will never be sold at the same price as a pint of ice cream on ECreamery.com. A brand new-Volkswagen bug will never be sold at the same price as the hottest new Jaguar. A Samsonite briefcase is never going to sell for the same price as a Louis Vuitton. A pair of Florsheim shoes is never going to sell at the same price as Gucci pumps. A Bic pen will never sell for the same price as a Mont Blanc.

Now there is nothing wrong with Good Humor, Volkswagen, Samsonite, Florsheim, or Bic. They are all fine brands and have their markets. But, if the mindset you have with regard to your product is in the realm of ECreamery. com, Jaguar, Louis Vuitton, Gucci, or Mont Blanc, why on earth would you price them like they were available at the Dollar Store?

Have a confident mindset. Your brand is the Jaguar of your industry!

What to Do with All That Money?

It may be hard to believe, but lottery winners are three to five times more likely to go bankrupt than the average American. How is that even possible?

Most lottery winners are completely unprepared for their sudden wealth. Many of them ignore advice from financial experts. They take all of the money as a lump sum, quit their jobs, buy a house, purchase a sports car, travel the globe, and recklessly *spend, spend, spend*. Oh yes, and sometimes fail to pay taxes. All of a sudden, three years go by and all of the money is gone; they've burned right through it.

If someone handed you $10 million, could you safely say you would be smarter than all of those people and have the right money mindset? Don't be so cocky: most of us aren't.

This also becomes a major problem when the business scales and money come rolling in. What do we do with all of that money?

Some business owners do everything right: They scale and win. In fact, they win big. The company grows to epic proportions. Wowee! Now it's time to buy that $100 million office building and $50 million warehouse they've been dreaming about. While we're at it, how about a few sports cars, a summer home, and an island in the Pacific?

I believe that we create our own limited world, therefore we have the ability to create an infinite reality. All we desire is possible.

—*Allison Maslan*

Don't get me wrong. It's fine to enjoy the fruits of your labor. You deserve every penny you've earned. Buy a new home if you've outgrown the old one. We bought our dream home last year. I love it even more because we earned every last brick and blade of grass.

So get a fancy new car, if you can afford it. Take a well-deserved vacation. At the same time, though, you need to be sure that your cash flow is strong, your Big Picture Vision remains front and center, and you have looked toward the horizon at what's coming next.

This is when a business coach – and perhaps a trusted financial planner as well – can be especially important to help guide you on the next phase of your life. Where should you invest your excess cash while leaving some reserves safeguarded? Should you sell the business? Or should you buy another one? Start building toward your succession plan?

There is also an opposite circumstance that can occur when a business owner starts to meet with some scaling success: *being stagnant.* These folks clutch onto their money tight and stay right where they are. They don't reinvest in the business or share any of the rewards with their team, their family, or their community. When this happens, life can be miserable for everyone involved. They might do so because they are afraid of losing it, are distrustful of others, don't feel they deserve the wealth or, well, are just plain greedy about hoarding what they've earned. Whatever the case may be, it's not healthy or productive for anyone.

> Every time you suppress some part of yourself or allow others to play you small, you are in essence ignoring the owner's manual your creator gave you and destroying your design.
> —*Oprah Winfrey , icon, media mogul, billionaire, and TV talk show host*

A friend of mine, marketing expert Alex Mandossian, has coined the term *cost of inaction*, or COI. This concept can be likened to opportunity cost. When you are stagnant on autopilot and refuse to take those bold leaps, you could be losing an absolute fortune. You will always say, "would have, could have, should have" when it comes to COI, but never when you have received the right coaching and taken calculated risks to grow your business.

Developing the right money mindset in anticipation of any situation that might arise is critical to your long-term scaling efforts, growth, and happiness. Whether you are a spender, a conservative hoarder, or somewhere in the middle, start shaping your mindset now.

For every success you will experience on the trapeze, for every beautiful trick that will gracefully catapult you through the air into the catcher's arms, there will also be numerous misses, overturns, overrotates, and painful plummets into the net. Each time, you will have the mindset that enables you to keep climbing back up that ladder, making that courageous leap, and flying through the air. Once you've achieved this, you will strive to do it better with even more grace. Then you will seek to fly higher.

You have the confidence, persistence, and stamina to scale your company and sustain it. Your determined mindset will enable your business to reach unbelievable heights, and you will create happiness throughout your journey in the air. It's time for you to fly.

Chapter Summary: You've Got This!

- DO work on improving your money mindset at every stage of growth.
- DON'T allow your emotions to cloud how you see your business.
- DON'T panic and quit – even when your business is caught in the eye of a massive storm.
- DO separate your personal life from your business entity.
- DO create and maintain a mindset of abundance.
- DON'T ever let your money stagnate.
- DO take the leap!

Conclusion

Once you have tasted flight, you will forever walk the earth with your eyes turned skyward, for there you have been, and there you will always long to return.

— Leonardo da Vinci, Renaissance artist and inventor

Congratulations – you now have all the tools at your disposal to grow your business from entrepreneurship to enterprise! You can fulfill your dream and scale your business as you have detailed in your Big Picture Vision. Nothing will hold you back – unless you think small, revert to old habits, or cave in to your emotions.

The Five Phases of Constructing a Self-Managed Company

As we've discussed throughout this book, your ultimate goal is to shift from being the boss to becoming a *leader*. Your end game is to remove yourself from the equation and build a self-managed company. Your role as the founder is to let go of the day-to-day, to strategize and build relationships to supercharge growth, and to inspire your team to achieve greatness.

I have shown you how to accomplish this through the Four Quadrants and ultimately by replicating yourself, so that you can devote your time exclusively to making a big impact with your Big Picture while adding in more play days to enjoy at your heart's content. The Five Phases, as I describe them, are another way of framing and summarizing the entire process.

Phase 1

This is your starting point. You run and rule everything in your domain. In fact, you *are* the domain. You create, implement, project manage, direct, coordinate, sell, and oversee every step in your company's process. At this stage, you are a *solo*preneur.

Phase 2

Your business is off the ground and you recruit a bare-bones staff. You may have an assistant, a marketing coordinator, and a bookkeeper. You've started to delegate a few things to keep people busy and earn their paychecks, but you are still reviewing and approving everything that comes in and out of your company.

Phase 3

Your business has taken root. You build a lean team consisting of talented employees in admin, finance, marketing, sales, customer service, and fulfillment. In this phase, you are:

- Clarifying your Big Picture Vision.
- Leading team meetings and sharing your Big Picture Vision.
- Collaborating with your team to create systems and processes.

As this is happening at a ferocious pace, you are simultaneously building a company culture and developing its core values. In all likelihood, you still have your hand in most decisions. You continue to review everything and perhaps undo and redo your team's hard work, causing churn and communication problems.

You may start to see your team feeling frustrated and unmotivated. They make mistakes and don't seem to take responsibility for their actions. This shouldn't be a surprise, even among talented employees: according to Gallup, over 70% of the US workforce say they are disengaged from their jobs.

Not to worry, however, because this is just a natural development phase that you are passing through.

Phase 4

This is where you realize you need to start trusting others so you can remove yourself from the day-to-day tasks. You recruit the *best talent* and/or *promote and train* team managers to lead the divisions of your company. You start to let go of reviewing and approving everything, empowering your team members to become solution oriented so they can step up as decision-makers. Your department heads stop acting like rule followers. They take ownership of their teams and become *leaders*.

You and your teams are now:

- Cocreating solutions.
- Brainstorming new opportunities and winning ideas.
- Showing up as thinkers versus clones.
- Empowering one another and building trust.

Your team members challenge themselves by asking these questions:

- How can we delight our customers?
- How can we innovate?

- How can we increase revenue and profit?
- How can we improve our systems and processes to save time and money?

As this transformation is occurring, you are focused on your Big Picture Vision and where your company will go next. Create extended products? Offer new services? Acquire another company?

In order to facilitate all this, you are coaching and mentoring your leaders and training them to do everything that you do. You are *replicating yourself*, so you can focus on these other business opportunities.

Phase 5

It's time for you to step back from meetings and resist adding your two cents to every discussion and decision. Lighten up the reins and allow your team leaders to run with their ideas and decisions.

It's difficult to let go so completely because you are accustomed to controlling everything. The company was your baby from the beginning, and your ego keeps telling you that only you know the best way to do handle things.

It is essential that you bite your tongue and resist the temptation to constantly provide input and/or have the last word. At this stage of the game, your team members don't need you. It's like adding caramel to an already great chocolate sundae. Yes, it might taste good, but the ice cream, hot fudge, whipped cream, sprinkles, and cherry-on-top are more than delicious without anything else.

You have superb leaders in place. You have systems and processes that work efficiently and are constantly improving. Your team is accomplishing great things independently because you trained them, trusted them, and empowered them. They are happy and are engaged in their jobs. You are no longer getting in everyone's way.

Meanwhile, you have moved on to your next business venture. You are taking Play Days. You are getting closer to achieving your Big Picture Vision.

Congratulations! You have *scaled your business.*

Principles Inherent to Scaling

Here are the top 12 principles to emblazon in your memory (if you haven't already):

1. **Don't be afraid to fail.** It's okay to fail – and you will at some point. Then you will recover and be smarter, stronger, and more resilient than ever before.
2. **Passionately believe in your Big Picture Vision.** Share it with your team, your customers, your partners, your friends, your family – anyone who will listen. Shut out the voices of those disbelievers. Don't allow them to throw you off your path.
3. **Always focus on ways to generate sales and keep cash flow going.** There are myriad ways to generate revenue to scale your business, including: Leveraging; Replicating Yourself; Hiring Forward; Upselling and Cross-Selling; Getting Customers to Buy More; Licensing; Expanding Globally; Franchising; Creating Certification Programs; and Buying Competitors. Find the ones that fit your model best and dive deeply with them on a daily basis.
4. **Invest in hiring your A Team.** Having experts to run the weakest of your Four Quadrants will free you up to focus on where you shine most. Make sure the people on your team are in the right positions and fit your company culture. Then inspire them to accomplish great things.
5. **Learn how to make quick decisions and stick to them.** I hope I've drilled this in enough by now!

6. **Delegate, delegate, delegate!** Get out of the way of your employees and empower them, so that your company becomes a self-managed one.

7. **Deal with the elephant in the room; embrace conflict to ultimately resolve it.** Practice saying "no" and setting boundaries, even if they might disappoint people. Remember: "*No* is the new *yes.*"

8. **Create and improve systems and processes that support and drive your Big Picture Vision.** Build your business through your systems – not your blood, sweat, and tears.

9. **Don't work with negative people.** Life is too short. Period.

10. **As the leader, everything bounces off you.** To grow your business to 10 times its size, you need to elevate your own personal growth and leadership by 12 times, to handle all that growth.

11. **Get support.** Stop losing opportunities and wasting time and money recreating the wheel. To reach your goals in a fraction of the time, work with mentors who have walked this path before you – and succeeded.

12. **Focus on creating abundance.** Constant worry about your finances can wreck your business fast.

The SCALEit Method: Your Never-ending Mission

As I've emphasized many times throughout this book, bad things will happen that impact your business the first time you scale, the second, the third … and, come to think of it, *every time you scale.* This is not negative thinking or by any means wishing bad things upon you, it's simply how things work in business and in life. Just as good fortune sometimes magically smiles upon you at just the right moment and saves the day, unfortunate events and circumstances occur at unexpected times as well. No matter how much you learn from your experiences and how hard you work to safeguard your business, unpredictable things always happen and somehow seem to conspire to derail you. The things that went awry with your first scaling effort might not be the same ones that happen with the second, the third, the fourth, the fifth, and so on. Or, the solutions that worked the first time don't succeed on the second.

The SCALEit Method outlined in this book should be in practice every time you scale. It's all too easy to become complacent and overlook or take for granted simple execution methods that could have prevented a catastrophe. Mistakes creep in because you and your team may have stopped paying attention or failed to notice that things changed or shifted since the prior scaling effort.

Each time you scale, ask yourself these questions:

1. Are you sticking to the Three Ps of Planning?
2. Do you write out Mile Steps and Mini Feats when beginning a major project?
3. When was the last time you examined and did troubleshooting on your systems and processes? Think of yourself as a mechanic working on your car: Have you done regular oil changes? Regular tune-ups? A 100,000-mile checkup?
4. Are you staffed enough for the next scaling effort? You may think, "Oh, I just created all of these new positions three years ago, isn't that enough?" But every time you scale, the work will increase exponentially and your resources need to be in place, trained, and ready to handle it.
5. Are you managing your time well? This is the easiest place for CEOs to relapse. Don't allow yourself to get sucked into handling minutiae!
6. Do your team members feel like entrepreneurs and owners of their respective areas? Don't assume they do, even if you feel you have this covered. Ask them!
7. Are you doing regular check-ins with your team? Again, you are not micromanaging. Things might be going

perfectly well, which is exactly what you want to see and hear. But you won't know unless you periodically engage in big picture check-ins. You are simply staying close to the business, knowing what is happening, and demonstrating to your team that you are paying attention and care about them.

It's easy for a business to become complacent. Don't ever settle for just coasting along, which leads to mediocre performance and flat results. Always demand the best from your team and from yourself. If your execution proves to be 100% flawless beyond a shadow of a doubt, perhaps it's time to take a day or two out of the office with your Big Picture Vision. If you have truly crossed the finish line with it, then it is time for you to think big and … create a new Big Picture Vision!

Parting Words

Remember Apple's brilliant "Crazy Ones" commercial from 1997? Can you name the twentieth-century icons who appear in it? The list is astounding, primarily because all of the figures continue to stand up to the test of time: Albert Einstein, Bob Dylan, Martin Luther King Jr., Richard Branson, John Lennon, Muhammad Ali, Mahatma Gandhi, Buckminster Fuller, Thomas Edison, Jim Henson, Maria Callas, Amelia Earhart, Alfred Hitchcock, Ted Turner, and Martha Graham.

To paraphrase the commercial and underscore its obvious point, genius is often mistaken as crazy and/or rebellious. If you want to "think differently" and produce something truly extraordinary, memorable, and lasting, do not let anyone deter you from creating your own trapeze in your business (or in your backyard). Do your thing, do it your unique way, do it well – and don't ever give up!

When I jumped into the beverage industry, I found that there were so many people around me saying that my ideas wouldn't work. For example, my company didn't use preservatives. I didn't realize that prior to Hint there were no water products that used our technology – heat. We pasteurize our product so that we don't use preservatives. I didn't want to use preservatives in my water.

I tried to network and talk to as many people in the food and beverage industry as possible for feedback. Everyone I spoke to at places like Coke and Pepsi – one executive, in particular – told me that my idea about being preservative-free was "just terrible."

These industry experts also told me that the way to do things was X and, if you went outside of that box, then you were never going to be able to do it. I encourage entrepreneurs today – no matter what industry you're in – to meet with and listen to those people. They have a roadmap and it's good to know what they think. But there are also times when you need to make your own decisions. In the end, I was so excited to hear that the executive from Coke was going one way because I was going another way.

—Kara Goldin, founder and CEO of Hint, Inc.
and keynote speaker

Scaling your business is one of the wildest rides you will ever take in your life. It gives you the opportunity to utilize your gifts and solutions to not only affect those around you, but to literally impact millions – and potentially billions – of people around the world. In the process, you will build an asset that can support your desired lifestyle for years to come.

Achieving your goals gives you an incredible sense of accomplishment. You are always challenged to learn a new trick (or business strategy) or to increase the height, rotation, speed, or timing of your current tricks (or tactics). However, to make that happen, you will experience hundreds of misses, falls, and complete fails. Without the fails, you will not experience the wins. They are a necessary part of the journey. They make those solid catches so much sweeter because you know you have earned every single jump by overcoming your fear, braving every twist and turn, and reveling in the *Yes, I did it!* sensation – regardless of the pain you experience along the way. Then recognize and celebrate all the tiny (and big) victories along the way. There are many more of these than you give yourself credit for!

To scale from entrepreneur to enterprise, be willing to take the leap. Otherwise, you will be stuck on the ground, looking up at the ladder, and always wondering what *might* have been – if only you had climbed.

One final thing. Since we've just mentioned John Lennon, I implore you to keep his profound words with you at all times: "Life is what happens to you while you're busy making other plans."

While you are scaling and meeting with success, pause and reflect on all the things that matter in your business and your life: your health, your family, your friends, your business network, your team, and your customers. Once you've learned how to live in the moment and enjoy it to the fullest, you can resume flying through the air with the greatest of ease.

Putting the SCALEit Method into Action

N ow that you have finished reading *Scale or Fail*, it's time to put the SCALEit Method into action so that you can benefit immediately. Here are five steps to implement now:

1. **Work as a team**. Share this book with your team, so they can support you to implement the concepts and processes In the SCALEit Method. Decide as a team which aspect of the method you need to work on first (Strategic Vision, Cash Flow, Alliance of the Team, Leadership, or Execution). Focus on one area per quarter. Download your bonus tools at: www.ScaleorFail.com/bonus.
2. **Put your plans in place.** Set your off-site quarterly and yearly planning meetings with your team. Use the tools discussed in this book to work through your challenges, plan solutions, and organize your execution and follow-through.
3. **Subscribe to my weekly program.** *Allie & You: The Business Success and Lifestyle Show* at www.SubscribetoAllie.com.
4. **Follow me on Facebook.** This can be found at: www .Facebook.com/allisonsfans.
5. **Get high-level support**. Founders and CEOs who create tremendous success have coaches. They do not do it on their own. Working with a business mentor and participating in a mastermind group is the smartest move you can

make for your company. Receiving this on-going direction and accountability will fast-track your success and remove the heartache and headache of running your company. Don't do it alone. Go to: www.PinnacleGlobalNetwork. com to learn more. Or, call 888-844-3550 or email us at support@allisonmaslan.com. Speak to one of our Business Mentors to see how we can support you.

6. **Scaling your company is not an overnight process.** It may take a few years to implement everything in this book – and even longer for the processes to become part of your company's infrastructure and culture. Work each aspect of the SCALEit Method and mindset on a daily basis and you will see dramatic growth within your company. Enjoy the moments that make up your journey and have fun along the way!

Acknowledgments

I feel truly blessed to be able to imprint my teachings, experiences, and insights on these pages and share them with those who are ready to make a big impact on this world. Bringing a vision into being is not a solo job. Thank goodness I learned early on that asking for help was a smart thing to do. So many loving people have supported me on the way.

I want to extend my deepest gratitude to …

The love of my life – my husband, Mike Rees. Waiting for me while I sat in a room to write for hours and hours on end, day after day, was not easy. Thank you for being my true champion. I did it, Babe!

To my daughter, Gabriella. I love being your mom. You are such a bold and beautiful soul with smarts and wits abounding. Be willing to leap into the unknown. That is how you learn how to fly.

I love you, Mom. Thanks for always being there and believing in me. Your strength and perseverance inspire me every day. You've encouraged me to write since I was a little girl. See? I listened!

Thanks, Dad. I have a sense that you have already read these pages as I wrote them. I would not be doing this work if it had not been for you. You taught me that, if I wanted something, I needed to go create it – just as you have before me. Thank you for passing on your stubbornness, passion, and determination. I wear them well, and I miss you every day.

To my brother, Jeff, and my sister, Wendy. Thank you for always being there, no matter what. I love you both. Jeff – hopefully this will get translated into Spanish!

Thank you, Susan, for being my best friend and soul sister all these years through all the ups, downs, and in-betweens. Your resilience and wise way of looking at the world helps keep my head clear and my feet on the ground. Love you, tons!

To my dear friend, Lori Stephenson-Strickland. Thank you for sharing your wise soul. I love being on this journey with you.

Here's to Colette Carlson for our endless happy hour talks that close the place down. You are such a gift in my life.

Thank you to my dear friend, Christine Rasmussen, for all of your love and support. You light up the world with your wisdom.

Thanks to my incredible Business Mentoring Team at Pinnacle Global Network. You are all lighting the world on fire with your big hearts and savvy business know-how. Thank you for being so committed to our clients and helping them grow, scale, and shine among the stars. We are in this together and I could not do this work without you. Thank you, Melissa Woods, for leading our team of CEOs so well. Our lives were definitely meant to be intertwined once again. Gina Ruby, Giles Fabris, Stewart Borie, Phil Black, Tammy Moore, and Chris Friend: You all rock – and that is a fact.

Thank you to Jennifer DeWitt, who is truly the greatest ninja of all time. You are such an incredible support to the team, our clients, and me, and you keep my brain on straight every single day. That is quite a feat in itself.

And Jared Salas, you have stayed the course with me all these years. Thank you for your endless creativity and dedication. You are the only person who worries more than me about the details of our events. I am so grateful.

Thank you, Robin Richter, for trusting me all these years! I so appreciate you.

Now, for my mentors and coaches …

Sid Wolf, you continue to inspire me from the heavens. I miss you tons.

Thank you to Markus Heon for being such a great coach and friend, and kicking my butt for 20 years in the gym and in my life.

Mark Leblanc, it's all your fault, and I thank you from the bottom of my heart for always being there.

Thanks to Cameron Herold, for believing in me and helping me grow; Joe Stumpf, for your generosity and writing the idea about Pinnacle on that infamous napkin; Joe Polish, for being the genius that you are; Michael Bernoff for being my brother from another mother and such a support in this wild and wonderful business world.

Richie Gaona, thanks for helping me face my fears, teaching me to fly, and saving my life a million times; Tamara Ogden, thanks for bringing out my glow all these years with your uncanny make-up talent, and Keith Munyan for sharing your photography finesse with me.

My gratitude to Gary M. Krebs, editor extraordinaire: thank you for helping me turn my work into words that I hope will be read for years to come. I am so happy I found you.

Thank you to my literary agent, Bill Gladstone, who has believed in me for the past 10 years. I finally wrote it, my second literary baby. I so appreciate your vote of confidence and *Scale or Fail* has found a perfect home with John Wiley & Sons. Thank you for inviting me to be a part of your enthusiastic and talented team.

To all of my incredible clients: it is an honor to be on this path with you. You blow me away with your courage. Thank you for your willingness to take the leap with me in the Pinnacle Global Network.

And, finally, to all of you who take the time to read these pages, may they lead you to your dreams so that you can get your greatest work out into the world.

About the Author

Author photo by Keith Munyan.

Allison Maslan has successfully built 10 companies from the ground up starting out as a single mom on her own. Today, she is the CEO of Pinnacle Global Network, her Business Mentoring and Mastermind Enterprise that is certified by Women's Business Enterprise Council (WBENC). She was recently called "the impressive entrepreneurial force that is Allison Maslan" by *Entrepreneur* magazine. She and her team of business mentors have guided thousands of business owners around the world to build high net-worth companies, double and triple their income, and create more passion and freedom on a daily basis. Her client list has included: Ben & Jerry's, Charlotte Russe, Supercuts,

Merrill Lynch, and Allstate. Allison is an international speaker and author of *Blast Off!: The Surefire Success Plan to Launch Your Dreams into Reality*, which was an Amazon #1 bestseller in the United States and Canada. She is a regular contributor to *Entrepreneur* magazine and executive producer and host of her own online television show, *Allie & You: The Business Success and Lifestyle Show*. Allison has been an expert guest on ABC, CBS, NBC, and Fox TV stations across the United States and has been interviewed for articles in *Success*, *Forbes*, and *Fortune* magazines. On a personal note, she has been a trapeze artist for over 19 years. She takes the leap every day, whether she is scaling her business or soaring high on the flying trapeze. Here she is on the flying trapeze: https://youtu.be/ uvBxhdsX-p8. In addition, Allison has also been a world-renowned homeopath for the past 20 years, which adds a unique whole person approach to her innovative business strategies and success roadmap. Allison is now appearing in an award-winning documentary: *Inspired by 11*.

Index

Page numbers followed by *f* refer to figures.